Love on the Mountain

The Chronicle Journal of a Camaldolese Monk

ROBERT HALE O.S.B. CAM.

SOURCE BOOKS

HERMITAGE BOOKS

CALIFORNIA

Library of Congress Cataloging-In-Publication Data

Hale, Robert.
    Love on the mountain : the chronicle journal of a
Camaldolese monk / Robert Hale. -- 1st ed.

       p.   cm.

    Includes bibliographical references.

    ISBN 0-940147-45-9 (trade paper)

    1. Hale, Robert Diaries. 2. Camaldolese--California--Big
Sur. 3. New Camaldoli Hermitage (Big Sur , Calif.) I. Title.
BX4705.H225A3 1999
271' . 14--dc21
[B]   99-38722
                                         CIP

ISBN 0-940147-45-9

A publication of Source Books and Hermitage Books
        P.O. Box 794
        Trabuco Canyon
        CA 92678

Printed in the U.S.A.

This book is dedicated to my brother monks of New Camaldoli Hermitage and Incarnation Monastery, and to our good oblates, friends and retreatants, and to all who value the monastic dimension within themselves. All of you have enabled me to write this chronicle. It has been written for you, indeed it has been written about you.

PREFACE

*None of us can really look at ourselves
except in the sight of God.*
FRANÇOIS MAURIAC *JOURNAL*

L ast week a very intense retreatant thrust into my hands
a manuscript and asked me to read it. It related his recent
personal history: his slide into deep depression and then slow
emergence through grace at the hands of many caregivers. The
pages sought to be a confession of faith and gratitude, written
for his family and for whomever else might read them.

I felt that certainly his family would be moved by his writing. It caused me to reflect that I do not possess even one page
of autobiography from my own deceased father, or mother or
brother or grandparents, or anyone else in my family. How valuable such writing would be to me! Then I started reflecting about
our own Brother Philip, who was the eldest monk at the Hermitage before he died recently: Brother Philip, who had been
here from the beginning, but who had not left us a single page
of personal writing. Towards the end we did tape some interviews of his recollections and reflections, but that is all we have
from him.

It occurred to me that though I have been a monk since 1959
and Superior here since 1988, I have written nothing, except in
a private journal, about my and our monastic life here. I did
publish a couple of books some years ago, and many articles,
but those were on topics of spirituality or theology. So, the
following is an attempt at documenting at least one monk's
experiences at the New Camaldoli Hermitage, how I see and
hear and feel the ongoing life of the community, and how I
encounter even the living God in this place. Writing it down
might be a help to others living here, and to people elsewhere,
in our common endeavor to ponder how the unfolding of our
life contains Life.

Christians, and perhaps monks in particular, have always
liked chronicles, because of our strong conviction that God is
working through our living communities, and beyond (especially

beyond). And so we have the great monastic chroniclers, Bede and Eusebius, and all the other medieval and early Church historians, harking back to the Acts of The Apostles, and further, to The Book of Chronicles and the Pentateuch, the very beginning of the Bible. Thus, Peter the Venerable 'chanted history's praises and lauded historians who transmit to future generations the things their own had witnessed.'[1] He berated the 'sluggish' who did not bother to hand down in writing what they have experienced.[2] And the twelfth-century monk-historian Ordericus Vitalis urges us all to 'sing' history like a hymn, in honor of the God of history.[3]

Christians have also honored the more personal, autobiographical genre, at least from the time of St. Augustine's *Confessions,* itself rooted in earlier autobiographical texts, back to St. Paul's personal passages in his letters to the first Christian communities. And all this in the conviction that the living God works not only through collectivities, but also in the individual histories of each of us.

What follows is a hybrid of chronicle and autobiography. The two tangle in my writing and experience, since my monastic community does mean a great deal to me, and given my duties as Prior. I hope what follows is not only the tale of one monk among monks, for the story of each person is to some degree the story of everyone. Even we monks, living such an exotic (bizarre?) life, might hope that there is a wider Christian and human significance to our joys, sorrows, hopes and fears. Raimundo Panikkar argues our case most boldly in proposing that

> ...the monk is the expression of an archetype which is a
> constitutive dimension of human life. This archetype is
> a unique quality of each person, which at once needs and
> shuns institutionalization. Such a conception has, I sub-
> mit, always been an underlying belief of tradition.[4]

No confidences are broken in the following pages; what is recorded is of the public forum—though some of the brethren and guests might wonder about the good taste of it all. But Priors do not have to have good taste. Often they are there to embarrass the brethren, to help them grow in patience! The first names used—Bruno, Isaiah, Raniero, etcetera, do refer to monks of the community. Friends and oblates are given their full name unless confidentiality is indicated.

After the date at the beginning of each section, the feast day or saint's day is given, if there is one. Our life at the Hermitage is deeply influenced by the liturgy, and so its seasons and feasts have importance.

We are Benedictines following the ancient *Holy Rule* of St. Benedict, and so we are part of the worldwide Benedictine Order. But as Camaldolese we are a specific branch of that great family, with our own emphasis on the contemplative, and on solitude along with community as a fruitful setting for prayer, meditation, spiritual reading, study, etcetera. Our architecture at New Camaldoli expresses this spirituality: the Hermitage consists of twenty-five small cottages, or cells, gathered around the three main community buildings, the chapel, library and refectory. And our schedule seeks to provide a balanced rhythm between moments of community and solitude, between prayer and work and rest. We gather four times a day for worship in community, at 5:45 A.M. for Vigils, 7 A.M. for Lauds, 11:30 A.M. for Eucharist and at 6 P.M. for Vespers. We also gather for lunch, but breakfast and suppers may be taken either in common or in the solitude of the cell.

Our hope is that all this can be taken as one kind of model for other Christians to ponder—just as their rhythms of life challenge ours. Certainly we all need balance between moments of prayer, work and rest, between community and solitude, speaking and silence. So too we all need the witness to intense, ongoing love that family life offers, as well as the witness to service that Christian professional life provides. We feel that the various Christian vocations complement each other, and we can only grow by speaking together about their similar and dissimilar rhythms and shapes.

Hopefully, the above justifies this writing. It could be argued that if anyone should keep his trap shut, it is a monk—indeed a hermit—of a contemplative Order. And most especially a Superior. The monastic rule of thumb is a good one, that one should break silence only if one has something better to offer than the silence itself. Silence can offer a great deal indeed! Hopefully, the following will not break silence excessively, and will even sing a little, according to the desire of Ordericus, sometimes in the sadder chant of Good Friday, but often enough in the joyful cadences of Christmas and Easter.

New Camaldoli Hermitage
January 1996

JANUARY 6TH 1996
EPIPHANY

Epiphany: the Manifestation of Light. Bruno has a theory that our whole life is a passing from darkness into light, first with our birth, then every morning when we wake up. But also every instant of clear consciousness is an emergence from a kind of primordial dark chaos. And every experience of faith, of love, of contemplative prayer is a Magi-like journey into God's Light. Thus we are called, according to the Paschal invitation of St. John, to be 'Children of the Light.'

+

A good homily by John today, regarding the Abrahamic faith of the three Magi. They, like Abraham, risk all in setting out from the East. They look into the heavens for assurance and keep heading toward the mysterious manifestation of the Father's Will. They do not find it in the dark fortress city of Jerusalem; Herod and his religious and political cronies do not even go out to look at the star, let alone follow it. The royal court is threatened by the light, and it will call forth Herod's darkest violence. But the Magi travel on to little Bethlehem, which means, mysteriously, 'House of Bread.' So, we today need to muster up our Abrahamic faith and set out, not for the fortress cities of our own lives and time, but for our own Bethlehem, to be nourished by the Living Bread.

+

The Christmas decorations are coming down. Rather less to take down this year than previously because we voted in Saturday Chapter in early December not to have trees this year—not to *kill* trees, as our more emphatically ecological brethren put it. The issue came up spontaneously, the vote: thirteen to thirteen, so I had to break the tie. It seems to me we can decorate quite beautifully with just branches, and branches grow back. All the millions of trees cut for Christmas season (for many, simply 'holiday' season) perhaps should not be. Our decision not to cut a tree is not the most important witness we give, but I think it is a good one. We all do need to be more aware of the fragile

1

web of living things. God knows, humans have devastated that milieu quite enough. Yet, some of those thirteen who voted the other way think the Grinch has taken over here!

+

A dream about my mother, my brother and I moving on from the monastery of Camaldoli... I have forgotten to pack and make them go back so I can gather all my clothes and junk. When I awake, the dream makes me think of preparing to move on for the Kingdom (mother and brother are now up there!) Is the dream offering an ironic comment on how I should not need to pack so much, if anything, for that voyage? Much of American life is about accumulating stuff and things; but the Christian journey is about cutting back and stripping down.

I came across this from Wallace Stevens: " Life is the elimination of what is dead."

In the same vein, the woman from Big Sur who gave us the lovely baby-grand piano, now wants it back. She has found space for it in Monterey. The Lord giveth, the Lord taketh away. We do have a good upright in the Community Room, so our two or three pianists will survive.

+

Saturday Chapter, the weekly meeting of all the monks, was lively, followed by an informal discussion over breakfast in the kitchen. We are pondering the survey we conducted regarding where the U.S. monks see their long-term community, and where abroad they might volunteer to go for a year or more. Seventeen of thirty-nine respondents indicated that they were available, for a year at least, for one of our communities in Italy, India, Brazil or Tanzania. I had not anticipated such great interest. Should we take this seriously and begin to prepare one or another for, say, the Sacro Eremo in Italy (they could use additional monks!) or for the Ashram in India? It would take a real commitment; a good knowledge of the language, history and culture of the place. It would also take humility—we would not want to be going in to tell *them* how it should be done.

In this regard, there was an article in yesterday's *New York Times* about missions and the new lay approach (since Catholic clergy and sisters are declining in number). The article noted that the purpose of the missionary is to put himself or herself out of business as soon as possible, by empowering the local community in its faith and gifts.

We are considering sending volunteers to monasteries abroad also because we are so tightly packed here. There is hardly room even in the old Ranch House for candidates. A happy problem.

+

One of the Californian bishops, Pierre du Main of San Jose, has been here on retreat. He says this is his favorite place to 'get away into silence.' He is one of the deeper and more erudite of the American bishops, qualities which seem not to be exactly burgeoning among them...

+

A good talk this morning with Brother Zacchaeus. We looked at all the photos of his Solemn Profession of January 1st. They do capture something of the beauty of the celebration. On Monday he will be returning to his theological studies at John XXIII Seminary near Boston, and will pop up to our New Hampshire monastery when he can.

A few days ago I gathered many of the papers I had in my cell relative to the negotiations and first foundation of that monastery, Epiphany Monastery, and took them over to our new archives rooms, and gave them their own official box. They document all we went through to get that house going. It is exciting having an East coast presence, enabling us to bust out of the California ghetto!

+

A new vocational candidate arrived yesterday, sober and serious, with degrees from Columbia and Berkeley. High salary possibilities. What is he doing in a place like this? Though I guess we do offer a package which promises astonishing upward mobility and long-term security.

3

I received a moving Christmas card from one of our retreatants:

> The Hermitage has been such a source of inspiration and renewal for me. Last Thursday I heard the medical report that I have terminal cancer. Among my thoughts immediately following was a longing to spend some days in retreat at the Hermitage. If my health permits, I'll seek the opportunity. I ask for your prayers. With gratitude for providing the environment that has given me glimpses of heaven. May you be blessed. In Christ...

+

We run quite an inclusive refectory. Today at lunch, Bro. David Steindl-Rast was at my table, talking about three workshops he is preparing at the human potential/new-age center, Esalen, which is nearby. Four tables down, the President and his wife of the very Roman Catholic St. Thomas Aquinas College, with Isaiah, who has been involved in that College in one way or another. At another table were two members of a Big Sur pioneer family, being hosted by Fr. Bernard. The offspring of this family still shoot at dogs and hippies that stray on their land! It would have been much more interesting if these various guests were clustered at one table.

JANUARY 7TH
BAPTISM OF CHRIST THE LORD

Jesus, the Suffering Servant, stripped of everything but human flesh and weakness, is plunged by the tough prophet John into the dark waters of the divine Will, the divine Being. And so each of us must be baptized.

Here is a more creationist reading of Christ's baptism: he descends into the Jordan and sanctifies all waters which bathe and sanctify the whole world, which thus becomes his extended Body. Teilhard de Chardin would have liked that.

+

I have had intense dialogue with Monk x which has caused me much sadness and anger. One of the most difficult things about the Prior's job is dealing with people who, it seems to me, have quite a reduced sense of the common good, who are intensely focused on their own immediate desires. On the other hand, promoting the common good is part of my job description, and maybe there is more than a little egotism in my pushing that line. Perhaps I am not far from Monk *x* in this regard. In the end, however, someone does have to witness to the community needs and if, after consideration and consultation, it appears that I must challenge the man, then I must, however painful it will be. Merciful God, give me and him compassion!

+

We are here on this mountainside, looking out upon the Pacific, simply trying to live our baptismal vows: simply trying to live Christ's new commandment of Love. That is enough to keep us busy. One of our old, grumpy monks at the Sacred Hermitage in Italy, when interrogated by puzzled guests, "What do you do here?" is wont to respond sharply, "Well, I try to survive! Does that seem like a small thing?" And we can only survive by loving. That is why we are here.

We try to put Christ's first commandment first: to love God with all our heart, all our mind, all our strength, all our spirit. That is assignment enough for each day! Then, we try to live that second commandment, like the first, as a fulfillment, an extension of the first, in loving our neighbor as ourselves. That is our *Rule* and our *Constitutions.*

+

Here are a few of the people with whom I am in contact today.

Three of the younger monks in formation, Randy, Raniero and Benedict have begun planning together their possible Solemn Vows Eucharist for June. Now they are all pondering their letters to Chapter requesting acceptance for Solemn Vows. These are three very good men prepared to risk their futures with God—scary enough! And with *us.* That causes a twitch or two also. Loving God, bless and sustain their offering. Don't play hard to get with them!

An older, white-haired woman has been asking in the book store about our choir director, Cyprian, who "sings like a rock star!" She asks if we have photos of him. Mark just told me this when he came by to tell me that he had done the calligraphy job I had asked for. He does splendid work in lettering, drawing and ceramics, and he is one of the warmest guys around. He is 'just' a novice, but seems very committed to the community. It is a joy to think of him here for good.

Then we have Arthur, our professional painter, preparing the seventh landscape for his upcoming exhibit at New Masters Gallery in Carmel in February. That will be exciting. God sends us some very gifted people. And those with less evident gifts are at least as important to the ongoing life of our diverse community.

Therese Gagnon, our older resident oblate, is also our resident feminist. Just now she was expounding excitedly in the book store with Raniero about the Church of the future, a Church that will fully accept women, a Church that will *dance!* No more the shame of the feminine, no more inveighing against the burden of mortal sins caused by women, from Eve on. That coming great Church will be such an explosive event, she insists, that the world might have to end in the ultimate Big Bang!

Some of the time Therese is angry, some of the time hopeful and exhilarated. She helps us remain aware that we males are not the whole of the Christian family, nor the whole of the human race.

+

Balance is extremely important for the Benedictine way. It needs to include both the feminine and the masculine. I would hope that one day ours here might be truly a mixed community. We have that in our own Camaldolese heritage, and certainly in the Benedictine and generally the monastic tradition. And sometimes in such mixed communities the superior was an abbess.

One does have to be careful regarding human nature, but permanent separation of God's two genders might not be the wisest way to be careful.

Another dimension of balance that I think we Camaldolese witness to in a particular way is that between solitude and community. It is there in the religious heritage, in the Bible, as it is in the yearnings of every human being. A person should not go into solitude to flee community, or plunge into community to flee solitude.

As I mentioned above, the architecture here at the hermitage expresses both forms of living. The cluster of individual cottages or cells gives space to solitude and interiority, *and* they are grouped around the three main common buildings; chapel, library and refectory, which provide communal living areas for the spiritual, intellectual and corporeal dimensions of our monastic family. Our daily schedule is intended to promote the same balance, as we move back and forth between the solitude of our cell and the community experience of our liturgy, meals, or other communal moments. Ideally, the solitude nourishes and deepens the community and vice versa. As the anonymous author of the medieval text *The Cloud of Unknowing* puts it, there should be a silence in our speaking and a speaking in our silence, and so too a solitude in our communal life and community in our solitude.

So, a Camaldolese hermitage recalls the ancient laura: a little monastic village, or a Christian ashram. As such it may be archetypal of any Christian community—or even of any individual. There seems to be a village within each of us, and it needs its chapel at its center, and a library, refectory and individual cells grouped about it. But whether the village is an emblem of the individual or of community, the whole Church must be present there too. Our Camaldolese monk, St. Peter Damian, who died in 1072, put it eloquently in his *Dominus Vobiscum*. A hermit priest had asked him whether, in celebrating Mass alone in his cell, he should say, 'The Lord be with you,' though there is no-one to answer. St. Peter Damian carries this specific, incidental question to a higher, theological and spiritual level (in the manner of St. Paul) insisting that the whole Church, indeed all the heavenly host, is there in the hermit's cell:

> The Church of Christ is united in all her parts by such a
> bond of love that her several members form a single body

7

and in each one the whole Church is mystically present; so that the whole Church universal may rightly be called the one bride of Christ, and on the other hand every single soul can, because of the mystical effect of the sacrament, be regarded as the whole Church... For indeed, although holy Church is divided in the multiplicity of its members, yet she is fused into unity by the fire of the Holy Spirit...And so it is good that whatever action in the liturgy is performed by any one section of the faithful should be regarded as the common act of the whole Church, joined in the unity of faith and the love of charity...and so although in our bodily solitude we seem to be far from the Church, yet we are most immediately present in her through the inviolable mystery of unity. DOMINUS VOBISCUM, CHAPTER V.

John Donne put it another way:

No man is an island, entire of itself; every man is a piece of the continent, a part of the main.
MEDITATIONS UPON EMERGENT OCCASIONS XVII.

+

Taking my daily walk down the hill, I was peering extra carefully at the glorious Pacific Ocean because this is whale migration season. Suddenly, I caught sight of two of them frolicking fairly close to shore. Thn they started just lolling about, mostly submerged, not breaching, and every now and then providing lovely spoutings. Native Americans feel privileged when such magnificent creatures allow themselves to be viewed, and I felt so. I remembered that delightful verse from Psalm 105, which we pray on Wednesdays at Vigils:

Yonder is the sea, great and wide
creeping things innumerable are there
living things both small and great.
There go the ships,
and Leviathan that you formed to sport in it.

+

We get some interesting retreatants and guests. Larry Fojtik has returned for a few days; he worked here as a young man for many months as he pondered what he wanted to do with his life. Now, still quite young, he is gambling on his creative gifts and going to art school in San Francisco, paying his way with a job as a taxi driver. He says when he is in his cab, especially at night he 'sees it all.' He has not been held up yet, and that is something. Hopefully God is particularly solicitous of such people.

Then Dennis Dunleavy is here on retreat; he is regularly down in Honduras, working with the poor. Often he comes here afterwards, to pray and ponder over it all—and make us more aware of the human drama beyond Big Sur.

The South American poor, the anguish of battered women, of people dying of AIDS—somehow we must be present to all people. If there is a God, our life of prayer on this mountainside might make sense. If there is no God, our life here is an obscenity.

+

One of the most respected American theologians visited us last week. The Vatican's latest edict against the ordination of women came under discussion. He said that it would take about a century, but that there would be Roman Catholic women priests. I felt anger and sadness. Either women can be ordained or they cannot. If they can, why does the Catholic Church have to wait a hundred years? If they cannot, it should not happen in a thousand. Plenty of eminent theologians, scripture scholars, canonists and historians are saying that there are no obstacles. The European theologian Karl Rahner thus held, before being taken to the Lord. What does he think now?

The issue is polarizing the Anglican Communion too. More and more of their national churches oppose the Vatican's position. A recent article in the emphatically R.C. *National Catholic Register* (not the *Reporter!*) argues that the Anglican move is why the Vatican felt it had to take action—quite before a theological consensus had been reached in the Roman Church—in order to block any kind of going along with the Anglican tide. But is the Vatican at its best when it is reacting against Canterbury?

+

Elected simplicity. 'To live simply that others might simply live,' (after Elizabeth Seton). That is a witness we monks can and must give, in the midst of obsessive complexity, conspicuous consumption, the throwaway culture. It can be argued that much of the Western market is driven by the stirring up of cravings, the creation of artificial 'needs,' the programming of early obsolescence. Madison Avenue requires that products be idolized, and then be made to quickly go out of style. Thus there is much spending, much cynicism, much sense of anguish and emptiness. To offer a prophetic 'No' to these darker aspects of a free market economy is to witness to the dignity of the human person who is called to be not just customer but saint.

+

We also try not to throw away or hide our elderly. Our infirmary cell is in the middle of things, as close to the chapel and library and refectory as possible. The elderly incarnate our history, bear the heritage, provide the family's memory. They cannot produce or do much, and that is their shame in the modern world. But monks cannot produce or do much either. The elderly have simply honed that skill of being able to do nothing really significant, and if they should happen to be less skilled in this way, physical and mental decline thrusts the facility upon them. If they can accept their condition humbly, God's past and future shine through their weakness.

JANUARY 8TH

Today I am taking my Desert Day. Once a month the brethren can have a day apart, each has the option of not coming to any of the community liturgies or happenings. It is a good time for going deeper within. Decades ago, in high school, I was terrified of solitude. I wondered if there would be any me there if I were not busily in the midst of the crowd. I have discovered there is plenty of me around at any time. The trick is to get beneath the me to the deeper wounded *i,* and the emptiness at the heart of the *i.* And in the tiny dark center of the emptiness, if one dares enter and be there awhile, amazing things can be found.

Our community is blessed with eight hundred acres of Big Sur coastal wilderness, and this morning at sunrise, while the brethren were singing Lauds in the chapel, I walked down the road and admired God's astonishing handiwork. The clouds were shifting colors from rose to pink to gold, the light blue sky was luminous, the ocean a palette of purples and blues. The color combinations were changing as the minutes passed, but every combination worked. The Impressionists and even a Turner have to carefully understate the things God does in nature in order to be believable.

+

There are three books I return to on Desert Days, and regularly at other times. They provide the foundation and framework of my personal prayer. The titles are; *The Cloud of Unknowing, The Way of A Pilgrim,* and Brother Lawrence's *Practice of the Presence of God.* That is all I know, and all I need to know. I first read them decades ago, as a college student or before. I knew Brother Lawrence's classic as a teenager and Episcopalian. As the years have passed, getting into the erudition game, I have branched out. But it is good for me to come back, humbly and realistically, to this core threesome of mine.

Now, to feed our need to be really serious, a critical edition of Brother Lawrence's little book has been published. In fact it is not altogether his book, but rather a collection of his letters and some interviews. This latest scholarly version would really amuse the good Brother.

I have to confess that I like playing around in the Middle English text of the *Cloud.* The full title alone is glorious:

The Clowde of Vnknowying,
In the Whiche a Soule is Onyd with God

That about sums it up: endeavoring to be Onyd with God.

The *Cloud* helps us in the key moment set aside exclusively for prayer. When we 'go into the inner chamber in secret,' as Christ exhorts us, and give ourselves as wholly and undividedly as possible to the Ineffable, then the *Practice of the Presence of God* helps us extend that contemplative prayer, at least intermittently, throughout the day (and even sometimes at night), in the various activities and pauses, ups and downs of our life.

Without the extended openness to God, the special, set-aside moments are artificial and forced. On the other hand, without those intense periods, it is not really possible to extend our daily communion with God in any deeper way. And the Jesus Prayer, proclaimed and celebrated in *The Way of A Pilgrim,* helps to tie both dimensions together, provides a 'golden thread' throughout our day and night, and helps us in the special moments to plunge deeper into God.

In little ways, the *Practice of the Presence of God* is conditioned by the seventeenth-century in which it was written, but essentially it speaks to the secular culture of our times. For God can be encountered anywhere, not only in the sanctuary or the sacristy, but also while driving down the freeway or while waiting in the grocery checkout, and also in the 'non-sacred' spaces of the monks' lives, here in the cloister. And as one moves into the secular regions of the heart, the spiritually 'non-appropriate' concerns, feelings, thoughts—God can be encountered even there. Whatever one's inner affective state one can acknowledge it, be there, and find the Living God in its deeper reaches. This larger implication of Brother Lawrence's work can free us from a lot of pious inner forcing and straining, as if we can only approach God when we feel terribly religious and the candles are lit. Here the Psalms help too—they turn any emotion, including the less cheery, and any situation, into prayer.

+

There was a thought-provoking homily by Louis this morning, on the Gospel about the casting-forth of an unclean spirit. Louis argued that though we might not be possessed by demons (let us hope not, though one or another of the brethren can be unpleasant sometimes), each of us knows ourselves to be possessed at times by dark forces stronger than our will, surpassing our capacity to control them. In those moments we should acknowledge in faith our need for a truly transcendent Power. We need the Christ to cast out our own destructive spirits.

One manifestation of these possessive forces, Louis argued, is our obsessive concern with the past or the future, our incapacity to simply be here, now, with the Lord who is present to heal. The present seems like a dangerously rushing stream, pulling us forward or knocking us backward, the *praesens fluens,* the rushing present of unredeemed time. But Christ passes through these waters and introduces us to the *praesens stans,* the standing salvific Now. In the resurrected Christ, standing before us, all time is present, baptismal, and Christ allows us finally to be free, to rest with him in a little foretaste of the Eternal Kingdom.

JANUARY 9TH
SAINT GREGORY OF NYSSA

Today's saint was a giant, 'The great master of Christian mystical theology of the Eastern Church,' according to an authority on early Christianity, Werner Jaeger. With his master, Origen, Gregory paved the way for the contemplative reading of Scripture.

The *Book of Exodus* is about a certain Moses helping a small people to escape from Egypt many centuries ago. In its fuller sense, the story also prefigures Christ freeing us from our own bondage, introducing us to the Promised Land of intimacy with our God. The authors of the ancient text did not foresee this further application, but what is in the conscious mind of the writer cannot be the only criterion for determining the significance of a text. Over time it may achieve a wider and deeper meaning. The mystics would insist on that. A Freud, a Jung, a T.S. Eliot would too. There is the *sensus plenior,* the fuller significance of whatever we write, say or do, or indeed, do not say or do. Only the Spirit can guide us into that fuller sense. Gregory, a Spirit-filled man, helps us take risks beyond the letter.

St. Gregory is one of those mystics of the darkness. In his classic *Life of Moses* he writes:

> What does it mean that Moses entered the darkness and then saw God in it? ...Leaving behind everything that is observed, not only what sense comprehends but also what the intelligence thinks it sees, the soul keeps on penetrating deeper,

13

until by the intelligence's yearning for understanding it gains access to the invisible and the incomprehensible...this is the seeing that consists in not seeing, because that which is sought transcends all knowledge, being separated on all sides by incomprehensibility as by a kind of darkness. Wherefore John the sublime, who penetrated into the luminous darkness, says, "No one has ever seen God."

[N. 162-163]

That is a kind of knowing that requires our full surrender. We like information that enables us to do things, to control data, to be more effective: the correct phone number that enables us to call Aunt Martha, the Web address that gives us today's stock market results. But to know God is to know no-thing, enabling us to do no-thing, only to stammer and to be astonished.

+

Our monk Raniero preached a delightful homily today. "I'm not just a cradle Catholic, not just born Catholic, I was Catholic from the moment of conception!" Then he traced his later credentials: parochial schools from the beginning, seminary high school, seminary college. "Somehow I got the message in all this that if I would just obey and observe norms A, B, C, D, then my immediate goal would pop out at me—bingo!— like a Catholic merit badge out of Sister's machine. And I'd have it. Then I'd go one step higher and observe norms E, F, G, H, and—bingo!— I'd have that more advanced merit badge. And it would all count up in heaven. Well, St. Gregory Nyssa teaches us that it is not like that at all. We're not after merit badges but the totally other God, and so our life is an adventure of passionate pursuit of the Beloved for all our years, and even for all eternity!" Not just a good report card, but divinization. And not just once and then it is done, but a Canticle adventure and pursuit that goes on forever.

+

Today, Newt Gingrich, Speaker of the House of Representatives, proclaimed proudly that the budget impasse could continue for months—and the stock market fell one hundred points! Talk about a powerful speaker! Where are our prophets who can thus shake the foundations? They, hopefully, are for the one Lord. It is not clear for whom Newt is speaking.

14

JANUARY 11TH
DECEASED FRIENDS

This is the day that the monks of our communities remember all our friends, communal and personal, who have gone to the Lord. Our young postulant who just lost his father, returned today from the funeral. As the only son, he had to work out many of the arrangements. He will have a lot to struggle with in the coming months and years.

We Christians have the astonishing conviction that our beloved dead are not cut off from us and from life, fatally stamped out, but rather are fulfilled. That does not take away the grieving. How great a void death wreaks in our ordinary experience! Yet I know that I am aware of the continuing presence of my own deceased mother and father and brother, be it ever so subtle, unobtrusive, usually unadverted, gentle like the softest light, but consoling and strengthening.

+

Our Chinese Fr. Joseph startled us today by showing up without his splendid beard, though he had left a moustache. A few zips of the razor, and a whole new face. He seems about ten years younger. This, after all, is one of the few privileges remaining to us males: the possibility of redoing our facial hair! His deeper motive is that he is preparing for a trip to mainland China and apparently beards are not the thing there. He does not want to call attention to himself in any way since he will be offering a class in the Patriotic Church while being available to the underground Catholic presence, which will involve some delicate footwork. Our dream is that this three-month trip to China, including Hong Kong and Taiwan, might lay the first groundwork for a Chinese monastic foundation years down the line.

+

I came across this entry in Thomas Merton's *Asian Journal:*

> What is important is not liberation from the body but liberation from the mind. We are not entangled in our own body but entangled in our own mind. [NOVEMBER 3RD]

This is a good corrective to so much anti-body stuff in Christian asceticism. Still, taken literally, the judgment is too simplistic, it seems to me. Certainly we can get entangled in our mind but also in our body (as Hollywood and Madison Avenue so well know), and, to use the fuller Patristic anthropology, get thoroughly entangled in our spirit. We can make a bloody Gordian knot of any and all dimensions of human experience. Only Christ can disentangle us, or cut through with the two-edged sword of his Gospel.

Thomas Merton certainly paved the way for many of us. I know he played an important part in my becoming Catholic, then Camaldolese. The last chapter on the Camaldolese in his *Silent Life* is a most eloquent and valid expression of our solitary spirituality. Years ago, one of our people here called Merton a fake. Interestingly, that person is no longer a monk or priest. Merton himself was at times something of a tormented soul, and, as he insisted, had more questions than answers towards the end. But they were good questions that point us beyond easy responses to the final Mystery.

Merton's questions opened him up to an astonishing range of interests; every important tradition of Christian spirituality, every major world religion, poetry, literature, and, last but not least, issues of social justice. He was a Renaissance man and a Trappist monk—quite a combination. In his Gethsemani hermitage he was able to go deeply enough into his own humanity, into creation, into their Source, so as to encounter everything.

+

At best, Patience can seem to be a soppy virtue, and at worst, a wimpy acquiescence to evil. But as our Daniel points out, at its best it is a true assuming of the human condition, a 'suffering with' (etymologically, patience comes from *patire,* to suffer). And so, authentic patience can be our way of 'filling up what is lacking in the suffering of Christ,' [Colossians 1:24]. Patience can help us to get beyond the fight-or-flight alternative, to open a way (though it be the Way of the Cross) into Christ's Paschal Mystery.

JANUARY 12TH
SAINT AELRED

Deep Christian friendship can be precisely where we discover the risen Lord. This is one of the important messages of St. Aelred. Jesus, in his decisive hour at the Last Supper, bestows this great gift upon his disciples: 'I call you no longer servants but friends.' The first Apostolic community, Aelred insists, was a community of friends:

> Were they not...strong in the virtue of true friendship, of whom it is written: 'And the multitude of believers had but one heart and one soul; neither did anyone say that aught was his own, but all things were common unto them.'[1]
>
> SPIRITUAL FRIENDSHIP, I:28

This interpretation of Acts, by the holy twelfth-century English abbot, is right in articulating a key intention of St. Luke himself, according to some Lucan scholars. Friendship was indeed the highest value of much of the Greco-Roman world, and Luke sought to proclaim that becoming a Christian would not suppress that value but would fulfill it. This is a powerful example of effective Biblical enculturation.

The Apostolic community, newly gathered and formed by the Spirit of the Risen Christ, should be the primary model for every Christian community—familial, parish, monastic. So, the Quakers are onto something: every Christian community should aspire to be a bond of friendship.

Taking friendship in its more rigorous sense, Aelred realistically notes that we cannot open ourselves in friendship to just anyone, because of the degree of trust and intimacy required. He warns against 'carnal friendships,' and counsels going slowly in moving toward friendship. But once it is shown to be authentically Christian and growing, one should persevere in giving one's best to the friend. And in the joys and sufferings of the developing bond, Aelred assures us, other virtues will be developed, the Christian life of both friends will mature. What *The Way of the Pilgrim* affirms about prayer, what St. Augustine affirms about love, Aelred affirms about friendship: be persevering, and everything else will take care of itself:

> In human affairs nothing more sacred is striven for, nothing
> more useful is sought after, nothing more difficult is dis-
> covered, nothing more sweet experienced, and nothing more
> profitable possessed. For friendship bears fruit in this life
> and in the next. It manifests all the virtues by its own charm;
> it assails vices by its own virtue. It tempers adversity and
> moderates prosperity. As a result, scarcely any happiness
> whatever can exist among humans without friendship...'A
> friend,' says the wise man, 'is the medicine of life'...among
> the stages leading to perfection friendship is the highest.[2]

I like Aelred's point that Christian friendship should not be
sought as a means to overcoming loneliness (there is so much
of that around—in the Hermitage too!) and certainly not to
expand one's power-base, or build a clique, or something like
that. Christian friendship, as *agape* lived and reciprocated, is
an end in itself. The good abbot writes:

> Spiritual friendship, which we call true, should be desired,
> not for consideration of any worldly advantage or for any
> extrinsic cause, but from the dignity of its own nature and
> the feelings of the human heart, so that its fruition and re-
> ward is nothing other than itself.[3]

Friendship is one of the highest and noblest of our
experiences also in our time. In a competitive society that can
become a jungle, in our anonymous megalopolises, often enough
the one thing that can save a child, or an old person, or even the
middle-aged, is friendship. Some of the best contemporary
novels and films are about redemptive friendships. It is for these
reasons that St. Aelred speaks directly to our time.

Aelred traces friendship back to its ultimate source: the
Godhead. Our Divinity is not some kind of impersonal, gigantic
monolith, but a communion of Persons bound in one friendship
love. That is the import of the doctrine of the Trinity.

Aelred himself has to be pushed and nudged to this insight
by his good friend Ivo.

> *Ivo:* What does all this add up to? Shall I say of friendship
> what John, the friend of Jesus, says of charity: 'God is
> friendship?'

Aelred. That would be unusual, to be sure, nor does it have the sanction of the Scriptures. But still what is true of charity, I surely do not hesitate to grant to friendship, since, 'He that abides in friendship, abides in God, and God in him.' [4]

How can we imagine heaven? A friend of mine, quoting Sartre, I think, said he had no difficulty whatever in imagining hell, but could not conceive of heaven! Well, one way might be to focus on friendships, one's intimate relationships, and then try to imagine them extended to more and more people, and then imagine all this without the grievings for others that friendship demands (in sickness, suffering, death, for instance). Aelred proposes this very model: heaven is where finally we shall be able to love all with the one friendship love of God; and thus the gentle English abbot ends his marvelous book:

> Then, with the dispelling of all anxiety by reason of which we now fear and are solicitous for one another, with the removal of all adversity which it now behooves us to bear for one another, and, above all, with the destruction of the sting of death together with death itself, whose pangs now often trouble us and force us to grieve for one another, with salvation secured, we shall rejoice in the eternal possession of Supreme Goodness; and this friendship, to which here we admit but few, will be outpoured upon all and by all outpoured upon God, and God shall be all in all.[5]

In his other important work, *The Mirror of Charity,* Aelred explores the nature of every form of love. Here too, he is tremendously helpful, especially because he traces Christian love back, not primarily to *eros,* passions, emotions or sentiments (though they all might be very much involved), but to the *will.* Certainly a graced will, hopefully a will that is heartfelt and sustained by warm affect, but nonetheless the faculty of will.

Christian love is not primarily about this feeling or that, but is rather about willing the deepest good of the other. Bene-volence, willing the good. We are very influenced by romanticism (not always at its best) in, for instance, its contemporary Country Western or Hollywood expressions, and so we feel that unless we are swept off our feet by love, it cannot be the real thing. This may be well and good for teenagers perhaps, but such a notion of love is radically challenged by the Gospel. We have to love everyone—As the little Italian mother of our Fr. Andrew puts it, "Tutti, i belli e i brutti," everyone, the beautiful as well as the ugly. Jesus insists that we must even love our enemy, not to mention those to whom we feel simple indifference. In such cases one is not swept of one's feet, of course, no rush of beautiful sentiments, no positive attraction whatever for the other. Nevertheless, as Christians we are called to love them all, that is, to will their final good, their fulfillment and beatitude.

What, then, is Christian friendship love? It is that benevolent love which is accepted, appreciated, reciprocated by the other, so that, as Aelred teaches, the two friends become in Christ, 'one heart and one soul.'[6] Spousal love is that same reciprocated love, with a much fuller part played by eros. Both these forms of love can stir up deepest emotions so that there is total communion.

But love of enemy or love of stranger, is still substantially love. It is just not repaid—at least often not in this life.

So, Christian love is also an ascetical challenge: to keep working on the will to benevolence is no easy thing. And our generation appears uncomfortable with the will. Many seem not to know that they possess it, and in its stead own to a series of sensual appetites that must be satisfied as soon as possible. The Nietzchian Will to Power does not help in validating the will. The answer is not to abandon will for appetite, but to reclaim and redeem the will for God.

Aelred's insights regarding Christian love, so powerful in their human application, have even greater bearing on the love of God. Many devout people enjoy for extended periods a palpable attraction to God and the attendant interior spiritual consolation, in short, a love that can be *felt*. When all this consoling spiritual sensation disappears, they *feel* they are no longer loving God, that they no longer *can* love God. This is precisely the moment when the deeper, more authentic love can begin. Chapter eighteen of Aelred's Mirror of Charity is entitled:

In What We Should Believe the Love of God Consists

And he observes in this regard,

> No spiritual person fails to realize that the love of God should be appraised, not according to these momentary

attachments which are not at all dependent on our will, but rather according to the abiding quality of the will itself. To join one's will to the will of God, so that the human will consents to whatever the divine will prescribes, and so that there is no other reason why it will this thing or another except that it realizes God wills it: this surely is the love of God. The will itself is nothing other than love... The will of God is itself his love, which is nothing other than his Holy Spirit by whom charity is poured out into our hearts.[7]

Aelred obviously is not just talking about doing things in a way that would be pleasing to the divine Will: proper Catholic comportment, or something like that. He is referring to the deepest union with God, wherein the Holy Spirit, 'The will and love of God' transforms the human will

...totally into the Spirit's own mode and quality, so that clinging to the Spirit in indissoluble unity, it is made one spirit in the Spirit, as the apostle teaches: 'Someone who cleaves to the Lord becomes one spirit with him.'[8]

+

As you might have guessed from all of the above, it was my turn to preach today, and I have given some attention to St. Aelred. And as some might further guess, my homily got a little long...

It was particularly embarrassing preaching with our own Fr. Aelred Squire present. He has done much first-class research into St. Aelred.[9] Still and all, our own Aelred has preached on this feast for the last five years, and it is good for him and the rest of us to shuffle the deck sometimes. He has promised me he will preach on my feast, St. Robert of Newminster, about whom I have been waxing lyrical for umpteen years!

JANUARY 13TH

Fr. Joseph Wong came to talk over final details with me about his exciting trip to Asia that begins next week. The truly significant part for us Camaldolese is that half of his time will be spent on mainland China where Camaldolese, in all our thousand-year history, have never set foot. He will be teaching a class, On The Holy Spirit in the Sheshan Seminary in Shanghai for over a month. Twelve hours of lessons a week. This is an Open Church seminary (one of China's largest), and among the sixty seminarians in his class there will be a variety of political positions and faith stances. As Fr. Joseph observes, with a wonderful Chinese wit, even if he is drawn into questions about democracy and freedom, the People's Republic of China is publicly quite as supportive of these values as any Western capitalistic society, so he shouldn't get into trouble. We *have* made arrangements for phone calls and faxes knowing that they might be attended to by others—a challenging and different world from our monastic life!

Then Joseph is to have a week in Beijing, visiting Peking University and Buddhist and Taoist temples. It would be exciting if he were to encounter Taoist hermits. The Taoist tradition includes the eremitical experience, but it is uncertain whether Taoist hermits are there or can be contacted. Maybe such mystery and inaccessibility is appropriate for hermits!

The trip is being sponsored and funded by the Ricci Institute, whose Fr. Edward Malatesta, s.j., is an amazing man, Johannine scholar and China scholar in one. He entered the Jesuits as a young man intending to be a missionary in China, but got sidetracked into Biblical studies and teaching at the Gregorian University in Rome. Only in his sixties was he allowed to begin focusing on China. And as if all this were not exotic enough, a few weeks ago he became a Camaldolese oblate here—the first Jesuit Camaldolese oblate in our history. He will be preaching our retreat this year, on Interiority in the Johannine Literature.

One of our dreams is to eventually have a Camaldolese hermitage in mainland China. Were things to develop there at all, as they have in Eastern Europe and Russia, with the efforts of Joseph and the advice and help of Fr. Malatesta and the Ricci Institute, then such might come to fruit.

+

Our good friend Fr. Scott Sinclair is back to give us a series of conferences on the Gospel of St. Matthew. Scott did his doctorate, on St. Paul's Christology, at the Graduate Theological Union in Berkeley, where I knew him. He is an Episcopalian priest, though, as he notes, much more admiring of the present Holy Father than many Roman Catholic priests.

His first lecture today was fascinating, expounding the genius of Matthew in keeping the Gospel rooted in the Jewish faith and experience, yet open to the new; Jesus as Jewish, as fulfillment of the Jewish Scriptures, but as an opening to a new Heaven and a new Earth with his resurrection. Hence we are anchored in the Jewish heritage (we are children of Abraham) and at the same time open to the unexpectedly new. We should be able to bring out from our treasure new things and old.

Scott also stressed Matthew's exhortations to the new leadership to minister solicitously to the last, to sinners, and not to fall back into the righteous exclusivity of the Pharisees, for the young Christian community is composed of sinners, and several passages address the leadership particularly as sinners. Then Scott pointedly asked if some Church leadership today might not be slipping back into the exclude-the-sinners-from-our-holy-assembly mode. I wonder whom he was referring to? I guess the Archbishop of Canterbury.

+

The central place of the will for St. Aelred has caused me to take in hand again Gerald May's *Will and Spirit: A Contemplative Psychology*. May, a psychiatrist who is devoting his attention now to spiritual formation through the Shalem Institute, uses contemporary psychological categories, but also knows the Christian contemplative tradition pretty well, and he achieves some interesting conjunctions. He notes how will can go very bad, becoming simply the willfulness of ego,

...the setting of oneself apart from the fundamental essence of life in an attempt to master, direct, control, or otherwise manipulate existence. [10]

On the other hand, when the deeper self wills to open to God, then,

...that willingness implies a surrendering of one's self-separateness, an entering-into, an immersion in the deepest process of life itself. [11]

He notes how demonic willfulness can become, as we have seen in our own time, quoting Hitler's boast that he had achieved the new Germany 'merely with my fanatical willpower.'[12] The decisive thing is whether will is loving or not, and here he quotes his brother, Rollo May,

Will without love becomes manipulation.[13]

But when one abandons ego for one's deeper self and begins to love God, that is the royal road leading to contemplative union. Here he offers his favorite quote from St. Teresa of Avila, and it sounds like St. Aelred, and even more like *The Cloud of Unknowing:*

The will, however, is entirely occupied in loving, though it understands not *how* it loves. [14]

Fascinating, to jump back to medieval England and see how there and then the will is central, and precisely as faculty of love for the author of *The Cloud.* Phyllis Hodgson, in her scholarly introduction to that work, affirms that,

Love in *The Cloud* treatises, like 'intent,' is an act of the will.[15]

And she quotes from an important source of *The Cloud,* Ruldolph of Biberach, the flat-out affirmation,

Love is an act of the will *[amor autem est actus voluntatis].*[16]

Thus, for *The Cloud,* the will is our 'principal spiritual faculty.'[17] But of course it must be gently guided into the way of love, not degenerate into grasping willfulness, to use May's language. Or to use the striking language of *The Cloud* itself, the will must become the 'naked intention directed to God alone,'[18] and most directly in this exhortation of *The Cloud:*

Humbly trust the blind stirring of love in your heart. Not your physical heart, of course, but your spiritual heart, which is your will.[19]

And quite as emphatically:

> Follow eagerly this humble stirring of love in your heart. It
> will be your guide in this life, and will bring you to bliss in
> the next. It is the substance of all good living, and without
> it no good work can be begun or completed. It is nothing
> else but a good will directed to God...This good will is the
> substance of all perfection.[20]

There seems to be a consensus in the English School of con-
templative prayer regarding this path of the loving will into
Godhead. James Walsh s.j., in his scholarly notes to the Paulist
Press edition of *The Cloud*, mentions a parallel passage in Walter
Hilton's *Scale of Perfection:*

> The knitting and fastening of Jesus to a man's soul is by a
> good will and a desire for him alone.[21]

And Walsh goes on to praise Julian of Norwich for

> Her teaching on the goodly (or godly) will, since she ap-
> proaches it with much greater theological precision than
> either our author [of *The Cloud*] or Walter Hilton. [22]

Walsh quotes this definition of contemplative prayer of beseeching from Dame Julian:

> Beseeching is a true and gracious enduring will of the soul,
> united and joined to Our Lord's will by the sweet, secret
> operation of the Holy Spirit.[23]

Interesting, this quality of enduring which Julian indicates.
It is not a sometime affair. And it is possible with the will (at
least the graced will). Again, one cannot always feel this or
that, or hold this or that idea, but always one can, with the grace
of God, stir up a meek, naked act of the will that is beseeching,
loving. (Julian seems to take the enduring character of the will
in God very far indeed, beyond what the others of the English
School are thinking, but I would rather ponder the whole delicate issue later).

Here I think of that other great master of my own life of
prayer—so modest in his resume and station—Brother
Lawrence. He is just saying what the mystics are saying, but in
simpler terms. So, whether it be *The Cloud* or Walter Hilton or
Dame Julian or the Russian Pilgrim or Gerald May or Brother

Lawrence, each is trying to point to the one great possibility and calling: abiding in God.

That we can thus rest in God anywhere, anytime, no matter what is happening around us, no matter what is happening within us—that enduring capacity of deep prayer which is simple love, that is our catholicity, our universality in its ultimate, even its eschatalogical sense. That is how we shall be with God, and with one another, in the fullness of the Kingdom.

We can always love. Or, as the Russian Pilgrim would note, we can always breathe.

Back to Dame Julian and her understanding of the 'godly will.' Perhaps her most startling passage on this theme in Chapter 53 of the long text of the *Showings:*

> In this revelation I saw and understood very surely that in each soul which will be saved there is a godly will which never assented to sin nor ever will, which will is so good that it can never will evil, but always constantly it wills good and it does good in the sight of God.[24]

Oh my! One does wonder what the powerful and conservative Cardinal Ratzinger would say about that! Dom Roger Hudleston's critical judgment is not surprising:

> This is wishful thinking and not the teaching of the Church.[25]

But as I noted above, Walsh emphatically defends Julian's 'godly will,' and insisting on her great 'theological precision,'[26] he spells out his defense in his Introduction to the Paulist Press edition of the *Showings*. He notes her closeness to the teaching of William of St. Thierry, and quotes the last Julian passage regarding the 'godly' or 'goodly' will, which sets that will in Christ:

> All the lovely works and all the sweet loving offices of beloved motherhood are appropriated to the second person, for in him we have this 'goodly' will, whole and safe forever, both in nature and in grace, from his own goodness proper to him.[27]

For me, Julian can be thus defended, for she is using contemplative language that is radically open to Christ, presupposing our real incorporation in Christ. And certainly Christ's human

Will (not to mention the divine) 'always constantly wills good and does good in the sight of God.' It is Christ's Will that is the ultimate ground of our Christian will.

Christ's Will is to cleave to the Father. Our great High Priest, risen from the dead, always glorifies the Father. Here is the ground and substance of our 'constant prayer,' and when we pray deeply, and (a little more) continuously, we are simply entering into an awareness of Christ's prayer, Christ's Will, Christ's union with the Father.

Our contemplative willing of God is not a clenched-teeth intense determination to get God, in the way that an ambitious careerist might focus his or her energy in climbing the corporate ladder. Rather ours is a quiet acceptance of God's mysterious acting and willing in our lives. To use Twelve Step language, it is a letting go and letting God. Or, in Zen parlance, a kind of non-willing.

The willing-to-not-will paradox is explored in Chapter 34 of *The Cloud.*

> For this is the work of God alone, deliberately wrought in whatever soul he chooses, respective of the merits of that particular soul...Since you will it and desire it, obviously you already have it, yet it is not your will or desire that moves you, but something you are completely ignorant of, stirring you to will and desire you know not what. Please do not worry if you never know more than this, just press on with the exercise more and more, so that you are always engaged in it. In a word, let it do with you and lead you as it will. Let it be the one that works; you simply must consent with it...Do not interfere with it, as though you wished to help it on...It is enough for you that you feel moved in love...Trust steadfastly that it is God alone who moves your will and your desire: he alone, entirely of himself, without any intermediary, either on his part or on yours.[28]

January 14th
Second Sunday of Ordinary Time

I had a good talk at lunch with Scott, our visiting biblicist. He is writing a book on the messianic secret in the Gospel of Mark. Jesus comes as Messiah, but why does he want to keep it a secret? Why does he tell the people whom he heals not to tell anyone of the healing? I mentioned to Scott that years ago we were taught that Jesus knew his messianic role would be terribly misunderstood by the crowds—they were not ready to grasp its uniqueness, and only in the light of Jesus' suffering, death and resurrection could anyone begin to grasp the nature of the Messiah, the Suffering Servant who rose from the grave.

Scott said that he would more or less go along with this, but why does Jesus in Mark sometimes impose secrecy and sometimes not? The scholar argues that in every case secrecy is not exhorted, for example, in the case of Bartimaeus, or the people who carried the paralytic to Jesus, persevered in their faith, were insistent in believing in Jesus. This complete commitment would take them (at least virtually) with the Messiah to the Cross and beyond. Through their faith they already had some little share in the Paschal Mystery, however tentative and partial.

There are clear implications for us today. If we but persevere in believing, we have some insight into the Mystery, we can proclaim openly the Good News of the Messiah. Otherwise, we should shut up.

+

The Marcan persevering faith that leads into healing and the fullness of the Mystery is not unlike what the English Mystics were elucidating, albeit in their different language, about steadfastly willing God's love. 'All that rises must converge,' (Teilhard de Chardin).

+

Our ceramicist Mark really produces beautiful pieces. Yesterday he received a charming thank-you note from a woman who was on retreat:

Dear Brother Potter,

I want to thank you for the gift that one of your bowls has been to me while on retreat here at the monastery. It has been my companion in solitude, and I will carry it home to help me remember that I can return to my inner 'monastery' even when far from this mountain

In the crisp morning after Vigils, I fill it with hot milk and carry it to a bench to watch the sun rise. It warms my hands and tummy. After Lauds, returning to my room, I fill it with herb tea, rich with spices, and read for an hour Midday after Holy Eucharist, I place a scoop of rice and a big spoonful of curried vegetables in this bowl. Then tea in the afternoon and soup in the evening, always in the same bowl.

So you can see what a faithful companion your/my bowl has been and will be. Thanks be to you for your craft and thanks be to the Creator.

Blessings and peace, J—.

+

At Vespers we are continuing the reading of St. Paul's Letter to the Galatians. We have also had two ultra-Catholic visitors these last days, who like to intervene in the Prayers of the Faithful on behalf of Obedience to the Holy Father, etcetera. One of our more spirited fathers (Irish-American) immediately followed up one of their prayers for docile submission with a rousing (purported) prayer in favor of the Freedom of the Children of God! Thank heavens there cannot be wild cheering or hisses and boos in the context of the Prayers of the Faithful, but sometimes we come close. We do have a kind of applause meter, as one monk noted, in the intensity and volume of the response of the congregation: 'Lord hear our prayer!' When the petition is favorably received, the booming 'Lord hear...' can shake the walls; but when the petition is judged less felicitous the response can be almost silence.

All this is embarrassing, but what are you going to do? A few of our liturgical purists believe that the obvious solution is to suppress the spontaneous Prayers of the Faithful. But many of us feel that it is a moment of the Spirit when we finally get beyond *just* set prayers, however noble, and open up to all God's people expressing their hearts to the Lord in assembly.

Regarding liturgical purists, a bit of whimsy has been making the rounds: Question: How do you distinguish a liturgist from a terrorist? Answer: A terrorist will negotiate.

+

A Catholic cathedral ecclesiastic, articulate and cautiously progressive, is here on retreat for a week. At table today he was involved in some entertaining verbal sparring with our Anglican guest, Fr. Scott, about things Vatican. Our Catholic champion argued that the next pope might well be...different from the present one. He cited the example of della Chiesa, Archbishop of Bologna, on Cardinal Merry del Val's black list, blocked for many years from the Cardinalate, who ended up succeeding Pius X as Benedict XV. Then, of course, there is the example of Roncalli succeeding Pius XII. It is not the case, he argued, that a pope is able to determine who comes after him simply because he has named most of the electors.

The ecclesiastic proposed an alternate way to establish the College of Cardinals—to be constituted, in his view, not at the whim of the reigning pope, but at the decision of the presidents of the Episcopal Conferences throughout the world. Thus, episcopal collegiality would directly shape the College of Cardinals. It all sounded interesting to me, but I asked whether this would mean only one representative from large Conferences such as France or Brazil, with one representative also from small Conferences such as New Zealand? He did not have an answer to this, which surprised me. But he says that in ecclesiastical circles much thought is being given about where we can possibly go from here. The thought of more of the same is somewhat...challenging.

He also mentioned that he meets once a month with his Episcopalian counterpart to talk shop, compare notes and to spiritually and humanly support each other. I find that hopeful, and wonder how much quiet, behind-the-scenes ecumenical dialogue is going on.

+

Was it Ronald Knox who said something to the effect of, 'If you want to voyage in peace on Peter's Bark, stay out of the pilot-house?' Monks and contemplatives especially should not get too entangled in *le cose della Curia Romana.* They should not even jockey to sit at the Captain's table.

+

Scott, our Anglican New Testament scholar, was provocative today, taking his point of departure from Matthew's concern over even the first generation of Church leaders. What more striking juxtaposition, Scott asked, than Jesus affirming to Peter: 'You are Peter, and upon this rock...' and then, just a few verses later: 'Get thee behind me, Satan!' Scott then reflected on his being in St. Peter's Basilica, seeing the noble inscription inside the cupola: 'You are Peter...' and in splendid Latin, but not that follow-up verse.

Then Scott went on to muse that the Basilica itself expresses Matthew's fuller point: for it is the most expensive church in Christendom, so much so that it played a significant part in rending apart Western Christendom, with Tetzel preaching indulgences in Germany to raise money for it, and with Luther's horrified response.

+

The nearer we come to the truth, the more we must be on our guard against error.
THE CLOUD OF UNKNOWING, CH.34

+

When the French herald demands ransom of Henry V and his badly outnumbered troops, Shakespeare has the proud English king respond:
> The man that did once sell the lion's skin
> While the beast lived, was killed with hunting him.

In our world of hustling and huckstering, even in the specialized field of religiosity, there seems to be quite a bit of selling while the beast still lives.

+

Someone sent me a little card from the Anglican Fellowship of Prayer with the message on the back:
> Those who love God never meet for the last time.

+

Randy, one of our younger monks, just phoned from his folks' home in New Jersey. Each of our monks is permitted a couple of weeks a year with his family, and he chose this most challenging season to be back East—they are blanketed with twenty-four inches of snow and it is still coming down. His mother is a dedicated Catholic who taught most of her years in parochial schools, and two days ago Randy gave a talk to her church group, on prayer and his own spiritual monastic journey. He will return on Saturday (if there are flights) to continue his second year of studies at the Theological Union in Berkeley.

He loves the demands of urban monasticism, but also the very different rhythm of our Hermitage life here. Such is one of the unusual aspects of Camaldolese life: it has always embraced the gamut of forms of monastic life, from rural hermitage to rural monastery to urban monastery. If you can flourish in the more solitary form of the hermitage, here in the remote natural beauty of Big Sur, and also thrive in the bustle and distractions of Berkeley academia, then you have a certain breadth of spirit, which we find positive. Others might find it positively bipolar!

+

I phoned our New Hampshire house today, they are buried under four feet of snow, and it is still coming down. Vegetables are freezing inside the kitchen, along with the water pipes. God bless those East Coasters for persevering! Of course, they wonder about us Californians living in the shake and bake eschatolgical adventures of earthquake and fire. Question: How do you know rainy season has begun in California? Answer: The trees aren't on fire.

+

Then Cyprian phoned from his folks' parish in Phoenix, Arizona. He gave a concert of his own music there, and is offering a second tonight. Beyond that, he gave a talk on prayer to four hundred teenagers. Quite a challenge, he said, but he has been preparing for months, and he loves that kind of contemplative ministry with the young. Sometimes teenagers are more interested in prayer than their parents, and even their grandparents.

JANUARY 15TH
SAINTS MAURUS AND PLACID

Outsiders who know nothing about Christian (or Jewish) worship find our liturgies to be moving but very puzzling. For them, the Eucharist is a succession of curious happenings. So too is our Divine Office: Vigils, Lauds and Vespers. At Vigils, for instance, there are two lines of men dressed in white robes at 5:45 in the morning, tossing verses from some ancient (and often raw and 'primitive') text back and forth at each other The lines of men already know these texts, they have been through them countless times, so it is not a learning exercise; and it is not supposed to be a performance. So what is it? And why do it at 5:45 in the morning?

Well, it is at least something that Christians—and certainly Jews—have been doing together for untold centuries. The Psalms constitute the fundamental prayerbook of both faith traditions. I find it very moving to realize that in praying the Psalms, I and we here are united with countless worshippers throughout the world, down through the ages. And we Christians are united with our Principal Worshipper, Christ. The Psalms are about Him, and are about His prayer to the Father. So, in worshipping, we are not so much doing our own thing as entering into that one prayer of Christ, filled with the Holy Spirit, rendered to the Father.

Thus, liturgical prayer, like personal contemplative prayer, draws us into the very life of the Holy Trinity. Liturgy down here on Earth is a little foretaste and prefiguring of what we shall be doing, celebrating, rejoicing in, for all eternity. For ever and ever.

The Psalms as worship are God's Spirit-filled Word to us which we through faith make our own, and, united with the Word, offer in the Spirit back to the Father. The dynamic Trinitarian Cycle which is the shape of liturgy, of Scripture, of our whole lives as Christians, is of this nature.

Our own Camaldolese Fr. Cyprian Vagaggini explores this Trinitarian Cycle brilliantly in his *Theological Dimensions of the Liturgy.* [29] Our first retreat at the Hermitage, back in 1959, was offered by a wise Italian-American monk from St. Andrew's Priory (now Abbey) in Valyermo, California, Fr. Raphael Vinciarelli, o.s.b., who based all his talks on this work by Fr. Cyprian. And the retreat was splendid, certainly one of our best. It just may have saved my vocation.

I had come here having just recently swum the Tiber from sane and sober Anglicanism. At the time, the founding Father of New Camaldoli, Dom Augustine Modotti, God bless him, was urging some rather florid post-Tridentine Roman devotions, including Slavery to Mary.

I took my perplexity to the retreat master, Fr. Raphael, who reassured me that as a Benedictine I shouldn't worry about later devotions, certainly not about being a slave of Mary. I should just pray the liturgy and that would be quite enough. I found this counsel to be very reassuring because, as an Anglican, I was used to praying the liturgy. But not wanting to pull an end-run around my own superior, I returned to Dom Augustine and, in my own version of shuttle diplomacy, related, in softened terms, what the retreat master had said. Dom Augustine murmured something dark in Italian about such quasi-Protestant Benedictines, but from that time freed me from any obligation to even his dearest of devotions. And later I was actually able to approach one or another of those devotions more serenely, given that I was not being forced to them. (About my early consideration of an eremetical vocation, I write more below, especially in the entry for March 10th).

+

So I dedicated myself with renewed zeal to the liturgy. A main component of monastic (as of Anglican) liturgy is the Psalms. They provide, in Merton's words, our 'bread in the wilderness.' They turn every human yearning into prayer, and they also address the monastic yearning for efficacious prayer:

> May he remember all your offerings
> and receive your sacrifice with favor.
> May we ring out our joy at your victory
> and rejoice in the name of our God, [30]

and,

> O LORD, I love the house where you dwell,
> the place where your glory abides.
>
> I will bless the LORD in the assembly [31]

and,

> There is one thing I ask of the LORD
> for this I long
> to live in the house of the LORD
> all the days of my life
> To savor the sweetness of the LORD
> to behold the temple. [32]

The contemplative monastic life seeks to be about this, savoring the sweetness of the Lord...

and,

> I shall offer within God's tent
> a sacrifice of joy.
> I will sing and make music for the Lord.
>
> Of you my heart has spoken:
> 'Seek God's face,'
> It is your face, O LORD, that I seek. [33]

All of monastic life, all of Christian life, all of human life comes to that: seeking God's face.

Which reminds me of a wonderful aphorism of Dom Benedetto Calati, our former General. He would regularly affirm: "Before a man can be a monk, he has to be a Christian. And before he can be a Christian, he has to be a human being." That works not only chronologically, it is true at any moment.

Of course there are also those shocking Psalm verses of malediction. Our theology professor at Sant'Anselmo, Rome, (in the shadow of St. Peter's cupola!) once commented drily that he had no problem whatever applying each and every one of those ferocious verses! One does not quite know what he meant—perhaps it is better not to know.

I have to confess that I do not have great difficulty in applying such verses internally, spiritually. There are hostile forces within me that attack and compromise my personal and spiritual integrity, and so my spiritual life has also, alas to be warfare. These intense Psalm verses render all that as prayer, and very explicitly. In fact, the Psalms render *everything* as prayer. If we could but do the same!

A Zen Roshi, RebAnderson, gave a talk here on the Psalms: how he appreciated them for their flesh and blood concreteness. When you are angry, you are angry. When you are anguished, you are anguished. And all this, the Christian and the Jew might add, within the perspective of the LORD.

+

It was a lively conference today, given by Scott on the Gospel of Matthew and its disparate approaches to the Law, which range from frontal attack because it is too lenient (e.g., 5:21-48), to criticism that it is too heavy-handed (12:12; 15:11), and between the two, the Law is apparently affirmed as remaining unconditionally valid (5:17-18; 23:2-3). How are these different attitudes to be reconciled, the Law being a central reality in Israel's life and in ours? Apparently the author of Matthew felt that it could all be put together in one gospel.

Scott traced several lines of reconciliation: there might well be an earlier conservative Jewish/Christian substratum in Matthew, followed by a movement towards more progressive positions as the Church became predominantly gentile. Matthew is defending the little Christian community 'against' the party that had come to dominate Judaism, the Pharisees, hence many of the polemical lines. Matthew proposes God as the only norm for human life and conduct (5:45-48), but also acknowledges our radical weakness, insisting that Jesus has come precisely for sinners (9:13), and that moral demands cannot become crushing (11:30). At the center of all of this is Jesus who fulfills the Law, properly interprets the Law and gives believers the power to fulfill the heart of the Law. That fulfillment is in *love,* which sums up the Law, enabling us to distinguish what is central from what is peripheral (e.g., 12:12, etc.) 'When we lose track of love, we have lost track of the Law.'

The extremely radical demands of Jesus (for instance, to love our enemies, to turn the other cheek), bring us back to a realistic sense of our spiritual poverty and dependence on God. This is what prayer is also. This is the key to the Sermon on the Mount, and to Christian life: 'Blessed are the poor in spirit.'

Here again is a theological and spiritual teaching (indeed, as Scripture it is fundamentally normative) which rises, which converges with so much else for the Christian and contemplative life.

+

Every Sunday afternoon I phone Incarnation Monastery in Berkeley to talk to the brethren, see how things are going, to reaffirm the important koinonia between our two houses. They are so different: urban, small, cenobitical Incarnation, and rural, larger, eremetical New Camaldoli. But the same mysterious charism inspires both, both are emphatically Camaldolese, monastic, contemplative—and the brethren of both are bonded by real Christian love.

This time Andrew was away from Incarnation, involved in his ministry to the Italian Catholic Federation, but it was good to talk with Randy, just returned from his folks in New Jersey after a harrowing twelve-hour journey. I also spoke with Gregory, who is doing well, cooking his first meals for the brethren, getting to know the Graduate Theological Union library and campus before school begins in a few weeks.

Then I had a conversation with Cassian, who is still recovering from the flu, but mentioned that he wanted to speak more with Joseph Wong about his impending trip to China. He wanted to enquire just how broad an encounter with the Christian community there Joseph will in fact enjoy. This puzzled me, because Joseph will be there for several weeks, meeting over one hundred seminarians, the seminary faculty, other clergy, not to mention (we hope) Buddhist and Taoist monks. Not bad for a first visit, I would say. But I wanted to share some other news with Cassian, and let the subject go. And just today it occurred to me what Cassian might have been getting at.

He is one of our brethren who has intentionally decided not to become a priest, and to witness to the specifically lay character of monasticism from its beginnings. He, with others, is very attentive to signs of creeping clericalism in our midst, or indications of clericalistic presuppositions. So, yes, Joseph will be meeting with all those seminarians and seminary faculty and clergy. But what contact will he have with Christian laity in China? Interesting question. I put it to Joseph this morning, and he mentioned that he will in fact have some such encounters. But Cassian is right, one has not seen anything like the fullness of a Christian community if one has met only seminarians and clergy.

Yesterday evening we had a farewell party for Joseph in the community room, with munchies and soft drinks and beer and wine, and sang *For He's a Jolly Good Fellow!* He thanked us and asked for our prayers. The evening concluded splendidly with the video film, *The Lavender Hill Mob,* with Alec Guinness.

+

Speaking of sensitivity towards clericalism, our good friend and oblate from Big Sur, Penny Vieregge (who has taken the oblate name Damaris), prayed yesterday at the Sunday Eucharist Prayers of the Faithful that Church leaders would be tolerant and not controlling. Mamma mia! When I greeted her at the Sign of Peace, she laughed and said, "It just came out!"

JANUARY 16TH

Formation Team meeting this morning. The four of us gather once about every three weeks to review the men in formation: Isaiah as postulant master, Bruno as novice master, Raniero as assistant novice master (though he is still in simple vows), and me for the men in simple vows and those transferring from other orders. Just now we have nineteen men in formation, quite a good group for these days.

I am very happy with the four on the team. We differ from each other in many ways, so that gives a diversity of insights, and when we reach consensus it is reassuring. I think it is a very compassionate team, and no-one is on a guru-trip, no-one is trying to recruit disciples. The life itself is our principal formation program, and the Spirit the main formation guide. We just try to assist along the way, and not get in the way.

In our discussions we start from the latest entries on the list—the vocational retreatants and observers, (there are already eight tentatively on board for our postulancy class next December). Then we proceed category by category, with a mini-presentation on each man by the appropriate team member, followed by an open discussion of the insights, impressions and concerns of any of the rest of us. When we arrive at the 'level' of Raniero, he discreetly leaves, to avoid discussion about himself or his peers.

+

Bruno is just back from giving the annual retreat for the Trappists at the Abbey of Snowmass in Colorado. It has an exotic setting at eight thousand feet, with a fourteen thousand foot peak looming above.

The retreat seems to have gone very well. Their Fr. Theophane (the author) phoned here at its completion, praising Bruno to the skies, asking for any books or tapes by him so that they might have them for their library and carry them in their bookstore. John (in our book shop) told him about books and tapes by other eminent members of our community, but Theophane was interested only in works by Bruno. When things decline into a mere personality cult, it is very sad indeed!

+

Matthew's Christology was Scott's topic today. He traced the various 'titles' of Jesus. He spoke first of 'Son of Man,' with its messianic and kingly resonances, suggestive of Jesus' risen lordship over all things. (Matthew 28:19). Then we considered 'Son of Humanity.' That was a new one for me. I had always heard 'Son of Man,' even up in very inclusive Berkeley, but Scott (himself no radical feminist) insists that the Greek is not gender specific. In any case, Jesus through this title is a human being, a human being who has authority to forgive sins (e.g. Matthew 9:6), who will suffer (Matthew 17:12), and is also apocalyptic judge. And all these roles cohere.

For, what is the basis of Jesus' judgment and pardoning, but faithfulness on the way of testing and suffering? And what right has he to judge us? Because he, in the flesh, has been faithful in the way of the Cross. Forgiveness somehow presupposes comprehension, communion in the human condition. So, Christ's suffering and our suffering are right at the heart of Matthew's Christology. In this context Scott asked about the other religions: are they able to affirm a God or Ultimate Reality of some sort which truly participates in the human condition, in our suffering?

Then Scott explored the title 'Lord,' extending from mere societal salutation (such as 'sir') to reference to God, a substitute for the Divine Name.

And this was followed by expounding the narrative Christology: Matthew revealing who Jesus is especially through his ministry of healing, pardoning. This is where theology becomes life.

Scott, who likes to bring things together, suggests (with several other New Testament scholars) that these various aspects of Matthew's Christology are not hopelessly disparate, heteronomous, but rather that all can be gathered under the fundamental proclamation that in Jesus *God is with us*. This is announced at the very beginning of the Gospel (Matthew 1:23), and is proclaimed again in the very last verse as Jesus assures us, 'Lo, I am with you always' (Matthew 28:18). 'God with us' fulfills the promises of the Old Testament, all of which might be summed up, Scott argues, in the Lord's assurance that the time will come when he will fully dwell with his people. And it is a presence that means pardon and healing and reconciliation and communion.

Here again, we have in Biblical language what every monk, what every committed Christian, is trying to hear and live every day.

The author of Matthew was much challenged by the Judaism of the Pharisees, dominant in his time (between the years 85 and 90, Scott reckons). Faced by this form of religiosity, the author reacted, coming to the conclusion that, no, God is not approached most fully through a code, but through a person. The face of Jesus is the face of God.

The class concluded with the question: could it be that much of what goes wrong in the Christian life does so because we forget that we come to God through a person, not a code? This stirred up a fascinating discussion. How much of post-Tridentine Catholicism was understood as a call to righteous works, as a way to advance in virtue by obedience to regulations? Being open to a *person* is much riskier, more frightening, we noted. It requires entering into intimacy. And intimacy with *God?* Safer to follow some code! As if the most we can hope for is Parental approval. It is the way of love of Christ that leads to the very heart of God. Here again, Biblical proclamation becomes one with the contemplative journey. I think of Thérèse of Lisieux, setting aside her lists of all her good deeds of the day, simply abandoning herself to Jesus. Or the way of Teresa of Ávila and John of the Cross, of entering into the chamber of the spouse.

+

To suggest that the way into God is through a person also dramatically elevates the significance of one's relationship with every person. Our most revelatory 'model' for God is not the geographical one: God being the One, way up there in the heavens, we being down here on earth. Rather, we come to insight regarding God through human personhood—our own and others, for each of us is the 'image and likeness of God,' each of us the fathomless mystery of freedom, the capacity of wisdom and love in God.

JANUARY 17TH
SAINT ANTHONY, ABBOT

O nce a month I talk with my spiritual companion, not ex-actly a *director* in the post-Tridentine sense, but a friend with whom to talk things through and mutually discern the ins and outs of life. And my spiritual companion is a woman. In Berkeley I undertook the spiritual journey with a woman who was a wife and mother. Now it is Sr. Carol Marie Kelly, a Franciscan sister who has lived in solitude fairly close-by for some years. She has written books, given conferences, and guides many people.

We monks live in such a masculine world. First there is our monastic community here, which is all male except for Thérèse Gagnon, then there is the Church which is emphatically male-dominated, and then our society itself. Since the time I entered New Camaldoli (thirty-seven years ago!) I have lived in overwhelmingly male contexts, also when studying in theological schools, and then teaching. So it is a breath of fresh air to converse with a woman about deep things, and particularly good to journey with her, and sometimes to defer to her.

Just now that I am involved in this writing project, and have been for eleven days, I wanted to explore with her the relations between it and my commitment to my prayer and to the community. Because of her own contemplative writing, she is particularly helpful. We agreed that writing, at its best, can be prayer, can be of service to the community. At its worst it is an ego-trip. It is very helpful to keep focus on priorities, and mine are; 1) prayer, 2) community, and 3) this project—hopefully as prayer and community service, but not, therefore, to displace one and two.

+

While on the subject of women, I had lunch at a corner table in the refectory with a woman who is a doctoral student in Scripture, and a minister of the United Church of Christ. She is lovingly married and an emphatic feminist and is working on some classic spiritual issues, intensified by the world of academia and the heavy demands of her studies. Academia is its own world, with its hierarchies, laws, language and currency. The Christian can survive there, but will not necessarily thrive there without some real smarts, some real vigilance.

+

At Vigils we are doing a continual reading from the Book of Genesis, and today we were with Abraham as the alien in a foreign land. That land happens to be the Promised Land, where his progeny will become more numerous than the stars of heaven. On this feast of the 'Father of Hermits,' St. Anthony, I wondered if that foreign land is for each of us our own inner solitude. To journey therein is sometimes to feel alien in a foreign land. But there we can flourish.

45

So I will allure her: I will lead her into the desert and speak to her heart.

HOSEA 2:14

+

St. Peter and his role in the early community, was Scott Sinclair's topic for us today. All a bit delicate from the ecumenical point of view, and given that Scott is an Episcopalian. But he started off by acknowledging Peter's dominant role among the disciples—citing the evidence; that his name appears first in all the lists of the Twelve, that (in the Synoptic tradition at least) he is the first to be called, that he is given the keys, and so forth.

I had heard and thought about all this many times before, especially as an Episcopalian myself, pondering whether to go over to Roman Catholicism. But Scott also argued that Peter might have had a special influence upon the writing of Mark (Papias is claiming this in the second century), and in turn Mark had a great deal of influence on Matthew and Luke. What this means is that the first three gospels might have a petrine shape: many of the stories might have originated with Peter. When one talks about the stories of a community, one tends to relate one's own experiences. This point was new to me, and it causes me to feel a new reverence for Peter.

Scott argued that Peter also plays a theological and literary role in the Synoptics. He is a representation of every Christian, making the mistakes we all tend to make, asking the dumb questions and making the dumb comments we would all tend to offer. As such, he is the symbol of our weakness and sinfulness, the symbol of our lack of perception, lack of faith, lack of steadfastness. But the good news is that Jesus is always there, restoring Peter, literally pulling him out of the water when he is sinking. More than once Matthew emphasizes within the same passage both Peter's weakness and his importance through Christ's grace and commission. And so with all of us.

In class, I asked about the famous 'You are Peter and upon this rock...' passage—whether 'this rock' is the person of Peter, or the confession that Christ is the Son of God, or both: Peter confessing that Christ is the Son of God. The question was central to me when, as an Episcopalian, I was struggling with the 'Roman claims.' My rector was adamant that the Greek text was clear: Jesus was proclaiming the confession to be the rock, not Peter the person. However, Scott took the same position that my (Jewish) professor of Greek at Columbia did: the thrust seems to be that Jesus is pointing out Peter as the rock.

Of course, elsewhere Jesus confers the keys on the other Apostles, so we do need collegiality too (Vatican II's point). And Paul does not hesitate to rebuke Peter, as reported in Galatians 2:11. But even there, as Scott noted, Paul was not claiming that Peter had no authority, but rather that Peter was acting inconsistently, hypocritically. So, there is no getting rid of Peter.

+

Despite all our attempts at domestication, God deals in surprises.

MARGARET GUENTHER

JANUARY 18TH

Our first reading at Eucharist today was about Saul being furious because the women sang 'Saul has killed his thousands, David his tens of thousands.' Louis preached on the theme of recognition, how we all yearn for it, strive for it. Saul was just after recognition! Actually, he had it. It was just not to the same degree as David. That is where the old vicious poison of jealousy gets into the system. Louis pointed out that the comparisons between the two were fairly grisly: who had slain more human beings. And from Saul's jealousy, how many more deaths were to take place! How much of human history is made up of variations on the story of Saul's jealousy!

Louis noted that John the Baptist had quite a different approach: 'I must decrease, and he must increase.' Jesus himself sought to silence the evil spirits which recognized him, and even generally maintain the Messianic Secret. And he rebuked the adulator:

> Why do you call me good? No-one is good but God.
>
> MARK 10:18

We hunger for recognition because of our radical sense of alienation from community, from God. The gospel restores communion, if we can accept it, and then invites us to diminish the cravings in our ego, in order to manifest that all is from God.

+

Scott offered his last conference today, on Mary. He noted that the infancy narratives are not 'history' in our sense, but rather theology—the endeavor to understand, through prayer, pondering and searching the Scriptures, this first period of the Son of Man. But he added that he felt that this path likely opened up to Matthew and Luke (written almost one hundred years after the events) some basic insights that certainly accord with history— even in its generally accepted sense. For instance, that Mary and Joseph were exemplary in their lives, that they cooperated with God's plan, were not manipulated like chess-pieces on a board, that they were often puzzled by what was happening around them, that they remained faithful to the end. As such, they were the first disciples of the Incarnate Word, and primary models for us in our journey.

Scott noted that his own theological reflection in this regard remains tentative, but that various insights did seem to suddenly come together for him. He checked them out with his favorite theologian, Fr. Donald Gelpi, s.j., who encouraged him onward, and provided his incarnational theology, especially its basic assertion that God, by opting to assume flesh, accepted through the flesh the basic dynamics of the human condition. One of these dynamics is the decisive influence of the mother and father on the child. If Jesus represents for us the fullness of a whole and holy humanity, faithful all the way to God, then this has to reveal much about Mary and Joseph, about their spirit.

This is an ecumenical approach to Mariology that promises much for the future. Roman Catholic doctrines, Scott noted, such as the Immaculate Conception and Assumption, are not overwhelmingly evident in the New Testament, so when dialogue focuses on these issues, things can get difficult. He also noted feminist difficulties: Mary as the submissive slave of the Father, Son and (masculinist) Holy Spirit, does not exactly fill some theologians with enthusiasm these days. And some forms of Roman Catholic Marian piety leave many perplexed. Could such Marian devotions be sometimes compensating, Scott asked, for the virtual absence of the Spirit and the feminine in some ecclesiastical experiences?

To move beyond all this, it was proposed that we focus instead on Mary as an Ikon of the Holy Spirit. He suggested that the Spirit is 'the feminine dimension of God,' in that the Old Testament word for 'Spirit' is feminine, and the basic symbols of the Spirit throughout Scripture tend to be feminine: water, the dove, etcetera. The Spirit is the deep Wisdom of God (I Cor. 2:10-11), and a feminine figure in the Wisdom Literature.

Scott noted that when Mary appears in the gospels, quite frequently the Spirit is in the background, enabling the particular salvific event. Mary renders the Spirit visible. Thus, Gabriel announces to Mary that,

> The Holy Spirit will come upon you... therefore the child to be born to you will be holy.
>
> LUKE 1:35

When Mary then visited Elizabeth,

> Elizabeth was filled with the Holy Spirit and exclaimed with a loud cry, 'Blessed are you among women, and blessed is the fruit of your womb.'
>
> LUKE 1:41F.

In Matthew, Joseph is more than perplexed by all this. The angel of the Lord appears to him in a dream and reassures him:

> 'For the child conceived in her is from the Holy Spirit.'
>
> MATTHEW 1:20

In John, Jesus on the Cross gives to Mary the Beloved Disciple as her son, and gives to him Mary as his mother. A few verses later,

> He bowed his head and gave up his Spirit.
>
> JOHN 19:27;30

49

Scott said that nowhere else is that Greek phrase used, simply to indicate death; so the fuller sense must be acknowledged: Jesus is bestowing his Spirit as he bestows Mary on the Beloved Disciple, and him on her.

To appreciate Mary as rendering present the Spirit, is to open up possibilities for new insights regarding the feminine in God and Christianity, new possibilities for the lived encounter of all Christians with the Spirit, and with Mary.

All this quite evidently has implications for contemplatives.

+

At Vigils, we are reading the Sayings of the Desert Fathers for our second reading. Then, to offer some contemporary reflection, we are reading the chapter 'The Desert Fathers' from Simon Tugwell's *Ways of Imperfection*. It is wonderful to get back to the tough, foundational wisdom of the desert.

> What the Egyptian monks came to suspect was that ascetic and thaumaturgical prowess constituted a temptation as well as a public service...This is why, in Egyptian monasticism, enormous stress is laid on the virtue of humility. As Evagrius says, 'Asceticism with humility is valuable, but asceticism without humility is extremely dangerous.' And another Father said, 'It is better to fall with humility than to succeed with pride.' [34]

The thing to be concerned about now, as then, back in the Egyptian desert,

> ...is not isolated or even recurrent instances of sin, but a whole attitude of carelessness, of not facing up to what one is doing. 'Unawareness is the root of all evil,' as one monk said. [35]

In this age of billion-dollar industries of 'entertainment' and distraction, there is a lot of unawareness around and inside each of us.

> What the Desert Fathers are afraid of is a purely fanciful spirituality, quite unrelated to human reality. 'If you see a young man going up to heaven by his own will, grab his leg and pull him down again.' Going up to heaven just because you fancy it is not the right way to proceed. Unless there is a solid foundation of absolute realism, any spiritual high-flying will be liable to degenerate into illusion. [36]

Our good friend and oblate Marydith Chase has been here on retreat for several days. She is one of those women who is a powerhouse of contagious joy and enthusiasm. She is Pastoral Assistant of a huge Catholic parish in Bakersfield, California, and probably keeps the whole place going. This is one of the silver-linings of the shortage of clergy; the empowerment of very qualified laity. Another of our oblates was a Pastoral Assistant and, much to the delight of the priest, practically ran the parish. She is now working on an advanced theology degree.

Marydith has signed up our Daniel to go down to Bakersfield and give a week of conferences during Lent. I think parishes are, right after families, the grassroots Christian communities, and am glad of these bonds of friendship that we have with some. They keep us in touch with fundamental Christian realities.

+

One of our monks just telephoned from the hospital. He has had one of those exams where a tube with a light is pressed up into the colon to explore for cancer. The very good news was that there is none. He watched the whole thing on a monitor. Now he says he wants to preach on the text 'In the valleys of darkness I have seen a great light.'

+

The phone again. It is our good friend and oblate and attorney who does a great deal of *pro bono* work for us. After some legal stuff, I mentioned that one of her monk friends is on Desert Day today. Somehow we started discussing the monk's political views, which are definitely rightist. Early on, he shared with her a copy of the *National Review,* mentioning that he was given a life subscription to that periodical, and also that he was a long-time friend of William Buckley.

Others of the monks here are to the left of Mao. The exciting adventure is to keep the whole thing together. The oblate praised us for our charity and mutual tolerance in this regard. Also, when it comes to ecclesiastical questions, theology, spirituality, we do accommodate quite different points of view. Intentionally, we have not laid down an ideological criterion for entrance— only the fundamental one that the *Rule* offers,

that the candidate seems truly to be seeking God. Then, if one accepts Vatican II, our *Constitutions,* the *Rule of St. Benedict,* and especially the 'norming norm' of Scripture, that is enough. But it does take continuous work. Especially in an age (and in a Church) not known for tolerance and forbearance.

JANUARY 19TH
SAINT PETER ORSEOLO

The saint of the day was closely associated with our founder, St. Romuald, and is also one of 'the strangest of those recorded in history.'[37] Peter Orseolo, who was Doge of Venice, one night secretly left the city and began a journey to the Benedictine abbey of Cuxa, on the border of France and Spain. There he met St. Romuald, and under his influence, adopted a solitary monastic life. So, among other things, he invites us to ponder power and glory and wealth, the true kinds and the false.

As Doge, Peter had it all. But he somehow felt that he had nothing really. The inner fire and power of St. Romuald, of the solitary cell which he proposed (which in due course also attracted the Emperor Otto III), proved astonishingly stronger than all that the corridors of power could offer.

The first reading at Eucharist also plays with these themes. It presents the startling incident of Saul entering the cave 'to ease nature' as the liturgical reading delicately puts it. David and his men are in the back of the cave, and they urge David to take the opportunity, slay his enemy and seize the throne. But he will not. He feels guilty about even cutting off a corner of Saul's cloak, Saul being 'the Lord's anointed.'

Bruno preached, and waxed eloquent about the old, paranoid king, desperately holding on to his established power, crude and obsessed. He has neither grace nor freedom. He is the slave of his power. On the other hand, David, who is all freedom and grace, honors the anointed, because he is already virtually anointed himself. David is filled with surprises because he is not enslaved to the rule of power. This dialectic of the older and the younger is also seen with Isaac and Esau (about whom we are now reading in Genesis, at Vigils), and in another way by the older and younger brothers in the Parable of the Prodigal Son.

God turns precedence upside down and often favors the younger. Jesus himself, Bruno proposed, is the younger brother who is so threatening to the older Pharisees, Sadducees, Doctors of the Law, High Priests, Herod and the Roman authorities. All that power, all that establishment is threatened in a hundred ways by the Suffering Servant from Bethlehem, Son of David.

With Jesus, each of us should choose to be the younger brother, not grasping onto precedence or rights but aware that at every moment everything that matters comes as pure gift. This should be so in our encounters with others, in our public ministries and service, but also when we go within, to be with our God.

+

For about two years now, the solitude of my cell has been compromised by a cat, Elizabeth. She was born and spent her first month or so in the great outdoors. But our two dogs, Buddy and Scooter, were taking an excessive interest in her, so I felt I had to come to her rescue. I had never had a cat, except briefly during graduate studies. Ours was a dog family, and I was raised with the prejudices of dog-lovers, that cats are not affectionate, appreciative, and so on. It turns out that Elizabeth is a very loving creature. At the morning alarm (but not before), she jumps on the bed and we enjoy about three minutes of quality time together. Then regularly during the day we bond again. Just before lights out, she roars around the cell like a wild lion, only to quiet down for the dreams of the night.

There is a tradition, particularly in Celtic monasticism, of the hermit sharing his cell with a cat. I am glad of that, because sometimes I feel guilty about compromising the solitude of the cell. Having an affectionate cat about does not make for complete solitude. But she does remind me of the astonishing creativity of her Maker, who must be greatly involved in grace and speed and affection and calm.

Bro. David Steindl-Rast is a committed cat lover, and very appreciative of Elizabeth. He recently sent me the following poem by D.C. Berry:

On Reading Poems to a Senior Class at South High

> Before
> I opened my mouth
> I noticed them sitting there
> as orderly as frozen fish
> in a package.
>
> Slowly water began to fill the room
> though I did not notice it
> till it reached my ears
>
> and then I heard the sounds
> of fish in an aquarium
>
> and I knew that though I had
> tried to drown them
> with my words
> that they had only opened up
> like gills for them
> and let me in.
>
> Together we swam around the room
> like thirty tails whacking words
> till the bell rang
> puncturing
> a hole in the door
> where we all leaked out.
>
> They went to another class
> I suppose, and I home
>
> Where Queen Elizabeth
> my cat met me
> and licked my fins
> till they were hands again. [38]

Our artist monk shared with me another cat poem which dates back to the ninth century. It is apparently rather well known in Ireland in its original Gaelic, and concerns a monk chronicler and his cat:

The Scholar and His Cat

I and Pangur Ban my cat
'Tis a like task we are at:
Hunting mice is his delight,
Hunting words I sit all night.

Practice every day has made
Pangur perfect in his trade:
I get wisdom day and night
Turning darkness into light. [39]

+

It is all very well to commune with cats and dogs, and there are several of both at the Hermitage, but what about mountain lions, wild pigs, rattlesnakes, black widow spiders? We have them all here on our lands, to remind us that paradise is not simple. And how are the poor mice to relate to the cute pussycats?

About a week ago I was walking down the road at sunset, the colors glorious in the sky and on the ocean: time to commune with God's magnificent handiwork. Suddenly I spotted some critter, cat-like, but the size of our dogs, ambling ahead of me. I felt a rush of fear and stopped. We have had two or three sightings of mountain lions these last months, and I wondered if this was an older cub, with protective mother somewhere about. Perhaps it was just a large wildcat or lynx. In any event it would not be as friendly as my Elizabeth.

The romantic movement teaches us that nature is there to inspire and instruct. But the Native Americans knew that part of the instruction has to involve immense respect, caution and vigilance. There are some bloody claws out there in the shadows. Of course, there are bloody claws inside each one of us. It is one mystery of glorious creation fallen, struggling back to wholeness through the Incarnation. That enigmatic passage from Romans explores all this:

> For the creation waits with eager longing for the revealing of the children of God; for the creation was subjected to futility, not of its own will but by the will of the one who subjected it, in hope that the creation itself will be set free from its bondage to decay and will obtain the freedom of the glory of the children of God.
>
> ROMANS 8:18-29

It is all well and good to note the danger that nature poses to humans (yet are we not an integral part of nature?) but what about the much more terrifying threat that humans pose to nature? How many species are on the endangered list? And not because of mountain lions. When we don't slaughter them, we cage them, destroy their spirit. Rilke's early poem 'The Panther,' catches the tragedy:

> His vision, from the constantly passing bars,
> has grown so weary that it cannot hold
> anything else. It seems to him there are
> a thousand bars; and behind the bars, no world.
>
> As he paces in cramped circles, over and over,
> the movement of his powerful, soft strides
> is like a ritual dance around a center
> in which a mighty will stands paralyzed.
>
> Only at times, the curtain of the pupils
> lifts, quietly—. An image enters in,
> rushes down through the tensed, arrested muscles,
> plunges into the heart and is gone.[40]

We have wrestled for years now over the issues of wildlife and the wilderness. Being blessed with eight hundred acres of beautiful Big Sur coastland, we certainly have that obligation. In the early years we allowed a logging company to cut the woodland—for a share of the profits. And we allowed friends to come and hunt, in exchange for favors. But about eight years ago we set down some fairly rigorous principles: no hunting, no fishing, no logging. At most we can cut from our forest for our own heating needs, but not to sell the timber. Most of our cells have wood stoves, so wood is a basic fuel for us. We try to cut only dead wood or, at most, to carefully thin a section of trees. So, most of the Hermitage land is wilderness, with just our cloister area cultivated. Sometimes the natural balance seems to be tipped badly—too many deer, or too many rabbits, and then we are tempted to intervene. But so far, Nature has taken better care of herself than when we were extensively cutting and hunting and fishing. Our contacts with Little Bear and his Native American Center and with the Esalen Institute and with the Buddhist monks of Tassajara have influenced us in a very positive way in this regard. It is presumptious to think Roman Catholics are put on Earth just to teach others. We are here to learn.

+

The Big Sur hosts four large spiritual foundations, each quite different from the other: Little Bear's Native American Center, Windows to the West; Esalen, the rather famous Human Potential Institute; Tassajara Zen Mountain Center; and the Hermitage. For over three years we have been engaged in dialogue and have coordinated activities in defense of the Big Sur wilderness. To this end we established the Four Winds Council,

> To develop cooperative initiatives among the four centers and to promote deeper understanding and respect for the paths of personal and social transformation which each center represents. [41]

We had difficulty hammering-out the common Statement of Purpose. Esalen and Tassajara tend to be wary of 'God-talk,' but at the Hermitage, evidently, we are inclined to that sort of discourse, and Little Bear uses it in every other sentence. So some affirmations of a 'religious type' do creep in:

> We were all drawn to this area to...provide places of retreat and spiritual renewal.

On the other hand, there are long passages that sound somewhat 'New Age' to us hermits, but we went along with them because they can be interpreted in a Christian way. So, our joint purpose is

> To create places of learning for the larger culture...to explore the deeper dimensions of what it means to be a human

being; to learn and teach respect for the Earth, and to live in balance with her limited resources.

We really discussed that capitalized 'Earth,' but Scripture does affirm that all things have been created in and through Christ, their Head, so maybe we Christians can risk erring on the side of Creation for a change. The statement continues, regarding specifically the Big Sur:

> For us this land is a sanctuary, a holy place...For that reason we are taking an active role as advocates for this wilderness...Each center has the wilderness in its prayer and meditation. We are learning from one another and from the wilderness itself to deepen our spiritual awareness.[42]

From the Hermitage's point of view, this is ecumenism in its wider extension: embracing Gestalt people at Esalen and dancing Native Americans and zazening Buddhists, and the mountains and hills and shores and ocean of God's good creation.

+

The Four Winds Council has been involved in the recent local battle over a project for a new dam in the Carmel Valley, the construction of which would have devastated the land. Our means of resistance included showing up at public hearings and presenting statements, and especially participating in prayer vigils with Little Bear. The waters of the dam would have backed up over his ancestors' burial grounds, and further reduced the wilderness. The local press and much money were backing the dam. To our astonishment, the dam was voted down at the last election.

Now there is a development projected for the same beautiful valley, involving building a hotel, a golf-course and over a thousand homes. It is being booked as a conservation venture! We are raising questions. It is amazing how any area of undisturbed land is seen not only as a resource and challenge, but almost as an affront to the developers.

+

The more one converses with others, the more it is important to claim one's own heritage and to commend its best to those with whom one is in dialogue. Otherwise, one is simply a hanger-on, contributing nothing. There is an interesting article, 'Tracking a Spiritual Family History,' in the latest issue of the Episcopalian magazine, *The Living Church*. The author, the book review editor, notes that

> We have a spiritual heritage. As children of God, yes, but also as children of particular people in particular places at particular times...Philips Brooks once quipped that he was probably a Christian because of his aunt in Teaneck, New Jersey. Likewise, each of us is who he or she is through the incredible mix of genes, geography and relatives—blood or adopted. Attached to these particulars are often spiritual bequests. [43]

The author traces his own lineage back to the French Huguenots—but he stops there! That got my Roman dander up, and I typed off the following Letter to the Editor:

> Thanks for the stimulating piece...The author notes that our roots and heritage are important, and traces his back to French Huguenots. But before? My own male family line goes back through some stray Congregationalists in Massachusetts (from 1637) to sturdy Anglican stock in Hertfordshire, England. But before? Weren't our ancestors most likely Christians in communion with Rome, and back, generation after generation through the centuries? Isn't that the case with practically everyone whose people came from Europe? Isn't that the taproot and trunk of our own branch and twig? The point might seem tendentious, especially coming from a Roman. But the intent is to plead the point that if we want to value our spiritual roots and heritage, the Roman issue does seem to emerge again, and perhaps invites us all to persevere in the difficult but significant Anglican/ Roman Catholic dialogue, simply to know ourselves deeper.

They published another of my letters a month ago, so may decline the above, if only for that reason. One thing about Roman Catholicism, it is in a great many of us, deep in the bogs of the unconscious.

+

Deep grieving. It is surely one of the most difficult parts of the human experience. Today for Eucharist and lunch, we hosted a parish group of women who had recently lost their husbands. Our good friend and oblate, Joyce Bock, a Jungian analyst,

60

works with them at the parish of St. Angela in Pacific Grove. The women were very different from one another: one tall, thin, aristocratic, reserved —another, short, stout, chatty... But each had deep sorrow carved into her face—and an undefinable special human depth.

John preached, welcomed the women (as Joyce's group) and launched into a homily that was particularly helpful and appropriate. The first reading, quite providentially, presented David lamenting for Saul and Jonathan. The gospel reading treated of Jesus' family showing up and trying to take him away, fearing he had gone mad.[44] John noted that while the theme of grieving is evident in the David narrative, it is there also in the gospel: the family clearly grieving over Jesus' apparent derangement, Jesus himself undoubtedly grieving his family's lack of comprehension. And John argued that Saul had grieved until the day he died, grieving the decline of his regal power.

But, said John, there is a grieving unto death, a bitter grieving, and then a grieving unto life, which somehow brings peace. Saul's grieving is desperate, clutching, constricting. His power is ebbing away and he cannot stand to lose it. There is something possessive and desperate also in the grief of Jesus' family. They want to be able to take control of Jesus, to 'seize' him, or as a current translation has it, 'to take charge of him.'

Grieving unto death can be compared to moving into a small room: constricted, desperate quarters. David, who chooses life, does indeed grieve through public lament, fasting, weeping, rending his garments. But then he moves on to do his duty as the new king, enriched by his loving friendship with Jonathan, and even by his knowing Saul, his enemy.

And Jesus moves on, declaring (in another context) that whoever does the will of his Father is his mother, brother and sister. Grieving unto life, said John, quoting William Blake, is about moving on and into a more spacious room.

> He who binds himself to a joy
> Does the winged life destroy.
> But he who kisses the joy as it flies
> Lives in eternitie's surprise.

As I mentioned before, my spiritual director while I was at Incarnation Monastery in Berkeley was a wife and mother who herself had suffered great personal losses. She used to insist that grieving is one of our central tasks as humans. Every day is a losing, a dying, in many respects. But we contemporary Americans are so averse to grieving that we repress the central fact of loss. Ours is a culture of pleasure, an acquiring ethos, and our obligations are to be happy and to have. 'How ya doin'?' —'Oh, just fine!' Grieving is concerned with not being in control, not possessing any more, diminishing, dying. And none of that is quite proper or respectable. Not even patriotic.

Andrew, our Italian-American Prior at Incarnation, once asked me, "But in America, where are your cemeteries?" In his hometown near Milan, as throughout Italy, the cemetery is most evident, in a central place, near the community church. Andrew's mother visits his father's grave practically daily, on her way to Mass. Nothing morbid about it—just acknowledging his life with reverence, even his earthly remains, committing to his eternal life.

When we Americans do indulge in grieving, it is like taking up aerobics or something like that: steps to learn, motions to go through until we master it, obtain the benefits, and then hopefully get beyond the whole thing. But grieving happens, and we cannot take charge. The main thing is somehow to acknowledge the pain and to be there, and find a Presence at its heart.

January 21st
Third Sunday of the Year

One of the young monks here, on his first time leading the Prayers of the Faithful, let slip today a couple of non-inclusives: 'mankind' and 'men.' Raised eyebrows, uncomfortable stares from some of the monks and guests, delight from others. We try to use inclusive language at the Hermitage, at least when referring to humanity, but every now and then some 'sexist pig language' slips through—accidentally or otherwise. By now there does seem to be a majority of the monks on the side of inclusiveness, and certainly a majority of our guests are aware of the issue. But one of the monks calls it newspeak, and others suspect it is the beachhead of radical feminism.

+

Today's Mass readings were about those who lived in darkness and who saw a great light. Arthur gave a vivid homily about paintings, tapestries and morality plays—truly an artist's homily. He mentioned the Vatican Museum's immense Renaissance tapestries: one, The Calling of the Apostles, is bathed in light; then further down an immense corridor can be seen The Death of Peter and Paul, in darkest shades, yet the somber whole still expresses dignity and integrity; then there, in new sunrise brightness, is The Resurrection.

Then Arthur turned to the delightful Mexican morality play, *La Pastorella,* which he and Ed had seen a few weeks ago at Carmel Mission. Angels clad in bright white robes battle fiercely against devils all in black. The angels win the contest and condemn the dark demons to the fires of hell, to the relieved delight and applause of all. The scene changes to Jesus' birth, with Mary, Joseph and Bambino. Suddenly, the Holy Family, all three, are inviting the condemned devils to come up and celebrate the Nativity with them! And they do!

As Arthur commented, this is a delightful twist in the confrontation between darkness and light, and a striking way to present the power of the Gospel.

JANUARY 22ND
SAINT VINCENT, PROTO-MARTYR OF SPAIN

D aniel preached today on the theme of martyrdom. St. Vincent was terribly tortured before his death in Saragossa, in the year 304. Every martyr participates in the one martyrdom of Christ, who offers his life in love for each of us.

Daniel startled us by telling had known a martyr, someone who was terribly tortured and executed for his faith. Fr. Casimir Cypher was a Conventual Franciscan whom Daniel had met in

1974 at one of their houses of formation. Daniel remembers him as very witty and down-to-earth, not at all the 'pious Pollyanna.'

Fr. Casimir was later transferred to Honduras where he delighted in working with the poor. Apparently his arrest was a case of mistaken identity—the police were after a 'subversive' with the same unusual first name. In one sweep, Fr. Casimir and fifteen others were arrested. They were tortured and executed and their bodies were dumped in an empty field. The American Conventuals tried to secure Casimir's corpse for burial in the United States, but the clear evidence of torture would have been an embarrassment, and the Honduran government did not cooperate. The U.S. Embassy, often...involved in these things in one way or another, was not helpful either. So Casimir was buried in a Honduran church, San Germano.

Later, Daniel himself was on a mission to that country and, on Fr. Casimir's feast, was able to visit the shrine that had been erected in the church. Casimir is already virtually canonized in Honduras, with miracles reported. The faithful came on foot from thirty miles around, lighted candles at his tomb and celebrated their great saint.

+

One of our good friends is a nurse who directs his own care center for men in the advanced stages of AIDS. He regularly comes up here to rest, and consult about his spiritual life with one of our older monks. At the Prayers of the Faithful tonight, he remembered three by name who had recently died of AIDS. He barely made it through his petition, then started weeping.

+

Two of our men studying theology are also ministering to people with AIDS. It is part of their clinical pastoral training. Randy, stationed at our Incarnation Monastery in Berkeley, ministers at San Francisco General Hospital, world-famous for its AIDS care. Unfortunately, Randy is unable to develop an ongoing relationship with any patient because the hospital care is intentionally limited to specific intense treatments for short periods. Then the patients return home, or to a hospice—to die. So Randy just tries to be there compassionately for one stop on a short journey.

Our Zacchaeus, on the other hand, stationed at our Epiphany Monastery in New Hampshire, ministers at the AIDS-patient residence, Seton Manor, sponsored by the Archdiocese of Boston. There, the residents are dying, and one of Zacchaeus' friends, Harold, died last week. Zacchaeus describes Harold as "a black man aged forty-eight who did not look a day over thirty, and the sweetest, kindest, quietest person you could meet." He adds, "So you cannot escape death, no matter how much we would like to avoid it."

+

Gabriel's older sister died suddenly. He is away at the funeral. She was a Good Shepherd sister, and she lived a long and devoted life. It is good that he went to the funeral—he said to me, "We used not to do that here." One couldn't leave the Hermitage to visit a dying family member, or to attend the funeral. (But once a monk was flown home afterwards to sign legal papers!) Part of our *aggiornamento* is a recovery of the significance of the family, and of events such as marriages and funerals. That certainly fits in with our Italian heritage!

One of our young monks just lost his father a couple of weeks ago. He went home and had to organize many of the details of funeral and burial. The father had expressed the wish to be buried in the military cemetery, and the family and friends were concerned that it would be difficult with the congressional budget deadlock, and government workers on again, off again. But the funeral was able to proceed punctually. Thank heavens our federal government can at least provide burial for its military people.

Death does seem to be all around us. And, of course, within us. I have started pondering anew about my own death. I remember many years ago, I was sleeping in the divan in the front room of our family summer cabin, my brother Irv and sister-in-law in the one bedroom. The walls were paper-thin and I remember hearing Joanie confessing to Irv that she was worried about death. "Just don't think about it," was his answer. Not good enough, Irv!

When later he was struck with leukemia, Irv wrestled nobly against the creeping cancer and added some years to his life, important years for his coming to terms with death. When he knew he was close, he asked us from the hospital bed, "Tell me about the angels."

Monks are thought to be morbidly obsessed with death, and one or two are. But it is also possible to be obsessed with fleeing the thought of death. And it remains true that we can only live by coming to terms with our death.

The mystery of death is so immense that we can only wrestle with one aspect at a time; death as consequence of alienation from God the source of life, death as irreversible termination of all bodily function, death as terror of the psyche, death as fundamental challenge of the human spirit, death as being daily necessary to the ego, death as what every mortal must experience, death as making room for others, death as a return to Mother Earth, death as Christ's witness of love, death as narrow gateway to eternal life, death as Easter personally lived and celebrated.

At fifty-eight, going on fifty-nine, clearly I have lived out the majority of my years, and it makes sense now to be more aware of, and value more, the limited time remaining to me. That sounds platitudinous, and I do not have a foreboding of my imminent death. But my father died at forty-five, my mother at forty-nine, my brother at fifty-nine, so I am about to outlive everyone in my immediate family. To put it another way, they have anticipated my death, given me an example, lesson and witness, and also a warning and a reassurance.

Reassurance, because I do have a regular sense of their mysterious, subtle presence, supporting and strengthening me. And this with the presence of other deceased family members and friends. This is 'catholicity' in its greater extension: our communion with loved ones deceased as well as living, (and somehow even with those yet to come). In this larger perspective, the drama of death is made relative. It is simply the passage of one group of God's human family to another quite more favorably situated! But the passage can be a bit rough.

JANUARY 24TH
SAINT FRANCIS DE SALES

The Holy Triduum: Good Friday, Holy Saturday, Easter, is all about me, all about us, all about this central human adventure of suffering, dying, being reborn.

This paschal character of the adventure has a Trinitarian shape: to be a Christian is to come to terms with our death, and, sustained by the living Spirit, claim our mortality, surrender our whole being daily to the Father, knowing that in Christ we shall live anew. I find that the language and reality and experience of the Holy Trinity help very much here—it is only when sustained by the Spirit that I can move beyond terror and face up to my death and unite my dying to Christ's, becoming with him an oblation to the ineffable Father.

+

Today's gospel at Mass is about the sower who casts seed, and the birds get some of it, then the sun and choking weeds destroy more, but some seeds fall in fertile soil and bring forth much fruit. Isaiah, in his homily, offered us a christological reading, suggesting that the seed can represent not only the Word of God, but specifically Christ. For, he is an indestructible seed in history and in our lives, though threatened on all sides. So at the beginning of his life, Herod's soldiers swoop down on him like ferocious hawks, but they miss their prey. Later on, Satan tries "to shrivel him up in the hot desert, but that also fails." Then the crowds press upon him, threatening to choke him with so many concerns, but he survives it all, to go on to bear much fruit— "thirty- and sixty- and a hundredfold." [45] If we dispose our lives so that through our prayer and work and recreation we might be good soil, Christ will do the rest. But we need to be receptive soil.

Then, honoring the feastday, Isaiah offered these quotations from the gentle and kindly St. Francis de Sales:

> • Raise up your heart after a fall, sweetly and gently humbling yourself before God in the knowledge of your fragility: and do not be astonished at your weakness, since it is not surprising that weakness should be weak.

• When you encounter difficulties and contradictions, do not try to break them, but bend them with gentleness and time.

• The past must be abandoned to God's mercy, the present committed to our fidelity and the future surrendered to Divine Providence.

• If God has stripped us of the sense of His presence, it is in order that even His presence may no longer occupy our heart, but God Himself.

• (In all of these ways) the lead of our heaviness might be transmuted into gold.'

Christ is the great alchemist who can achieve this transformation, if we do not resist.

+

Benedict came to my place today with his letter requesting solemn vows. Written by hand, it traced in a very concrete and colorful way his path to our door, his conviction that God is calling him to remain with us till death. Randy, his classmate, has finished his letter and it is in the mail to me; and Raniero, the third of the group, hopes to finish his letter by this Sunday.

—Just a few pages of writing, but they express, after years of wrestling and discernment, the total commitment of the futures of three men. Talk about Paschal Mystery!

+

Fire is one of our major concerns here. The whole Hermitage almost burned down in 1985 as a huge forest fire practically engulfed us. We had to evacuate, most of the monks being hosted a little way up the coast at the Esalen Institute. Our younger monks helped their people fight the fire in that area. The heroic firefighters here kept the hoses spurting, and made back-burns, which efforts, combined with a providential wind, reversed the fire and saved this place on the Feast of St. Benedict!

With the arrival of the rains a couple of weeks ago, the fire season officially ended. But that does not mean we could not have a dangerous fire in one of our twenty-five cells, the majority of which have old wood stoves. And that is what happened last night. Matthew returned to his cell to find it filled with smoke. From the old stovepipe the ceiling had caught fire, just barely, but it was potentially serious. Using his trusty cell extinguisher, he put it out. But the place is a disaster area, with soot and chemical stuff everywhere—on papers, books, CDs. This is what our deceased Bro. Philip would have called 'a love tap from Our Lady.'

JANUARY 25TH
CONVERSION OF SAINT PAUL

From the Vigils Psalms, more verses that cut to the quick:

> O God, hear my cry!
> Listen to my prayer!
> From the end of the earth I call;
> my heart is faint

> On a rock too high for me to reach
> set me on high,
> O you who have been my refuge,
> My tower against the foe.

> Let me dwell in your tent for ever
> and hide in the shelter of your wings.
> For you, O God, hear my prayer
> grant me the heritage of those who fear you.

•

> So I will always praise your name
> and day after day fulfill my vows.[46]

+

Last evening we gathered for our monthly *collatio*, a communal reading of Scripture. We look specifically at the three readings of the coming Sunday Mass. Guests are also invited, and we sit in a big circle in the Chapter Room. The texts are read aloud and are introduced by one of the monks. Then anyone can contribute any thought, insight or question. Matthew, still recovering from his cell fire, went ahead and led this time (because he is presiding on Sunday). He said that he had made extensive preparation but all the papers had burned. Not true, but good for a chuckle. Then he suggested that we give more silence than usual to personal meditation on the text, then offer very short first responses. In a second round we were to propose more complicated thoughts, technical exegesis, and so on.

The gospel text was the beginning of the Sermon on the Mount from the Gospel of Matthew. Scott Sinclair, who had just given us conferences on that gospel, had argued that the first of the Beatitudes, being the first words from Jesus at the beginning of his public ministry, is the key to all his later teaching. So we examined that verse pretty carefully:

How blest are the poor in spirit: the reign of God is theirs.[47]

At least that is the official translation of the Lectionary. Our novice David, who did a doctorate on hermeneutics and liberation theology in Australia before joining us, had argued in Scott's class that the translation falsely 'spiritualizes' the beatitude, which would be better translated,

How blest are the poor *with the Spirit...*

thus focusing on a specific economic class, and emphasizing that the Spirit is with them. In class, Scott had opted for the first translation, which most exegetes have supported. David brought up the issue again during the *collatio* and provoked lively responses. Is his interpretation an ideological-political forcing of the text? Is the other reading a false spiritualization concocted to evade the hard social justice claims that Jesus and Matthew intended? Artillery and air attack and counterattack, and all in modulated, friendly tones! Many of the guests probably were not aware of the conflict, at least no one went ballistic!

John proposed a christological reading: who can claim to fulfill the beatitudes except Christ himself? He lives what he teaches. Hence, as we seek union with him, we can slowly begin to live the beatitudes from within. I proposed the mystagogical reading that Scott had suggested—to be poor in spirit is to have been stripped of all self-justification, self-reliance, self-righteousness, and to place one's whole hope in God. Hence the many references to Mary Magdalen, the sinners and tax collectors. And this is also the substance of contemplative prayer. Such a reading sees Matthew's version of the first beatitude as being immediately applicable to our relation with God. And if Scott is right, it is the substance of Jesus' entire teaching as given in Matthew.

The Gospel According to Luke, on the other hand, does propose the beatitudes in starkly social terms, as Jesus there proclaims simply:

> Blessed are you who are poor...Blessed are you who are hungry now...[48]

But Luke also has Jesus exhorting all to 'pray without ceasing.'[49] And the same gospel provides the striking scene of the listening Mary and the bustling Martha, with Jesus chiding,

> Martha, Martha, you are worried and distracted by many things: there is need of only one thing. Mary has chosen the better part, which will not be taken away from her [50]

But the heat of Christians and monks debating Scripture goes on!

+

A young writer who recently graduated from Yale is back on retreat, and last night we had a roaring discussion in the kitchen about...Scripture, among other things. How can Scripture be 'Word of God,' and give as exemplar one such as Elijah, who killed all those people in the name of Yahweh? Have we not progressed beyond that? I suggested that besides being the Word of God, Scripture very much consists of human words, that God's 'incarnation' in the written word involves a divine acceptance of the limits and constrictions of a historic writer and text. Every scriptural passage is not at the same 'spiritual level,' does not contain the same revelatory force; but the whole reveals an astonishingly patient God prepared to journey over the long haul with a little warrior tribe that at first can understand him only as their warrior god, who will defend them against their enemies and wants those enemies destroyed. But through the unfolding of this self-manifestation, God enables Israel to grow into the sublime insights and hopes of Hosea and Isaiah, of swords being beaten into plowshares and of all peoples worshipping the one God.

I am very energized by such discussions, and our back-and-forth exchanges drew the attention of other monks. But slowly, as the time passed and we two became the more absorbed in the issues, the others crept away, one by one.

JANUARY 26TH
SAINTS TIMOTHY AND TITUS, BISHOPS

Tonight we had our monthly poetry seminar. The format is more or less consistent: the poems are distributed beforehand, someone volunteers to present the poet being discussed, we take turns reading the poems and anyone can offer their reaction. This evening Bro. David again presented Rilke, whom he sees as a profound, mystical Christian, who felt increasingly alienated from the institutional Church.

This is the first time we have dealt with poetry that is not originally in English, so Bro. David had photocopied the original German of each poem, then, in two columns, the translations by Mitchell and Bly. He explored the German for us, its subtle allusions and double meanings, and noted problems with the two translations. It became clear that in each case we were dealing with three distinct poems. We came to realize that Auden was not overstating the case when he declared that poetry is what is lost in translation.

The poems we considered traced a spiritual teaching of great depth. How difficult it is for all of us to get beyond our busyness, our need to control! But when we can, what a sense of relief—even the experience of grace! The following reminded us of Eckhart, or the wisdom of Zen or the Tao.

The Swan

This laboring through what is still undone,
as though, legs bound, we hobbled along the way,
is like the wobbling of the swan.

And dying—to let go, no longer feel
the solid ground we stand on every day—
is like his anxious letting himself fall

into the water, which receives him gently
and which, as though with reverence and joy,
draws back past him in streams on either side;
while, infinitely silent and aware,
in his full majesty and ever more
indifferent, he condescends to glide. [51]

Bro. David noted that during a trip to Russia, Rilke was tremendously moved by monasticism there, and he entitled a collection of poems, *A Book for the Hours of Prayer.* In one poem a monk exclaims,

I find you, Lord, in all these things
fellow creatures I love like a brother;
as a tiny seed you rest in what is small
and in the vast you vastly give yourself.

Strength plays a marvelous game with things,
moves so servingly through the world;
gropes in roots and tapers in trunks,
and in treetops like a rising from the dead. [52]

This made us think of Gerard Manley Hopkins and his lyrical *God's Grandeur:*

The world is charged with the grandeur of God
It will flame out like shining from shook foil
It gathers to a greatness like the ooze of oil
   crushed...
There lives the dearest freshness deep down things... [53]

Then we looked into a wild Rilke poem, a brief Song of Songs about a desperate lover, about any passionate mystic seeking God, about the Bridegroom seeking us:

Extinguish both my eyes: I see you still;
Slam about my ears: I can still hear you talking;
Without my mouth I can implore your will
And without feet towards you I keep walking.
Break off my arms: I shall still hold you tight;
My heart will yet embrace you all the same,
Suppress my heart: my brain knows no deterrent;
And if at last you set my brain aflame
I carry you still in my bloodstream's flow. [54]

As dwellers in the Big Sur wilderness, we take a certain partisan delight in challenges to the self-sufficient city. But each of us is such a city, and each of us must pray that, with Rilke, we will have our foundations shaken,

> All of you undisturbed cities,
> haven't you ever longed for the Enemy?
> I'd like to see you besieged by him
> for ten endless and ground shaking years.
>
> ...
>
> He is the great Battering Ram
> and when he works he works in silence.[55]

This reminded us of John Donne:

> Batter my heart, three person'd God; for you
> As yet but knock, breathe, shine, and seek to mend;
> That I may rise and stand, o'erthrow me and bend
> Your force to break, blow, burn and make me new.
> I, like a usurpt town to another due
> Labour to admit you, but Oh, to no end
>
> ...
>
> Except you enthrall me, never shall be free
> Nor ever chaste except you ravish me.[56]

We rush about and sustain so many public roles and it is all rife with death. But all that time there is a deeper self timidly yearning only for God. And somehow that is our true self, where we perdure, where we are image of God:

> My life is not this steeply sloping hour,
> in which you see me hurrying.
> I am a tree before my background;
> I am only one of many mouths,
> The one that will be still the soonest.
>
> I am the rest between two notes
> which are somehow always in discord
> because death's note wants to push in—
> but in the dark interval, reconciled,
> they stay there trembling.
> And the song goes on, beautiful.[57]

JANUARY 28TH

Arthur hung his seven new paintings in the refectory yesterday so the monks could enjoy a preview before the exhibit next week at New Master's Gallery in Carmel. In the evening we held a reception with monks and retreatants invited and refreshments served. Mark and Matthew laid a splendid table with cheeses and crackers and a lively dip, champagne(!)and wines and sparkling cider (always important to offer nonalcoholic drink!) The refectory was crowded with monks and guests (some from Esalen), and Arthur happily mingling. I brought the camera and made like a press photographer. I pointedly asked Bruno if there had ever been an art exhibition when *he* was Prior. He replied immediately with dry humor, "No, because I didn't allow artists in!"

The paintings are amazing. They all depict the Big Sur coast, but each is quite different from the other. One is a sunrise, another explores especially the ocean and sky, with just a bit of jutting land. Another looks to the land, another is a sunset. Arthur uses very small but emphatic brush-strokes which create a special vibrancy in the views of sky and sea and land— certainly akin to the Impressionists, similar to Pointilism, suggesting Van Gogh, but still quite distinct.

Arthur also paints religious canvases (crucifixions, etcetera), but he clearly states that his landscapes and coastscapes are quite as spiritual as his explicitly religious work, and they do indeed have a contemplative quality. The Divine Creator seems to be just behind the scene.

We Camaldolese have always encouraged the arts. Lorenzo Monaco influenced Fra Angelico. A school of Camaldolese miniaturists at our Renaissance monastery in Florence produced beautiful manuscripts, now scattered to museums throughout Europe and the U.S. The New York Metropolitan Museum recently mounted an exhibition on Renaissance Florence, and Camaldolese artists were featured. I derive a particular joy from the presence and work of our contemporary artists—both here in the U.S. and in Italy. Grace and the monastic vocation do not repress God-given gifts, but encourage their fulfillment.

And so with the gifts of music. Cyprian gave a concert in Salinas the night before last, and spent yesterday in conferences on liturgical music and worship. His CD and tapes and sheet music are selling briskly across the country, and he has a new CD and tape about to come out. He loves Gregorian chant, but feels (perhaps with justification) that since we are not living in the middle ages but in the late twentieth century, our music should reflect that. His liturgical compositions are sober and careful, in the spirit of Gregorian, but when he composes and performs religious music outside the liturgical context, the lid comes off! Elements of Jazz, Reggae and Rock, Ballad and Blues get woven in. Not everyone likes it. But, like Arthur's work it is creative, unique and faith-filled. And it makes one want to clap and sing.

+

But what about monks who are not creative painters or composers? There's the rub! Our Camaldolese theology insists (as does the New Testament) that we all have important gifts from God. Some are more spectacular, some more hidden. It is a whole network of 'regular monks' with practical gifts which keeps the Hermitage going, day after day, year after year. A painting or a song—or a book, for that matter— doesn't get the food on the table, nor keep the generator running. We need mechanics (like Emmanuel and Isaac) and engineers (like Michael) and cooks (like Benedict and Rene) and bakers (like Steven) to make it through even one week. Actually, we need whomever the Lord sends us, and up to now the Lord has shown a lot of imagination in that regard. One monk commented that we are like the creatures on Noah's Ark, only instead of two of a kind, each of us is one of a kind.

JANUARY 30TH

What makes our dying alien and shakes us
Is that it's not *our* death, but one that takes us
Only because We've not matured our own.

RILKE

77

JANUARY 31ST
SAINT JOHN BOSCO

Bernard gave a delightful homily on the *simpatico* saint who would let his boys shout and run and carry on wildly, as long as they were basically on the right path. Apparently two priests wanted to carry him off to a mental institution. He ushered them into the carriage, slammed shut the door, locked it and directed the driver to gallop off to the institute with the priests within. They screamed so frantically that the driver and the institute doctors were convinced they were the intended patients. At least that is Bernard's story.

Then a militant anticlerical shot at John Bosco while he was teaching in the classroom, the bullet pierced only his sleeve, and he exclaimed in mock indignation: "My best cassock!" After that a dog would mysteriously appear to protect the saint from other anticlericals.

With a touch of embarrassment, having recounted these tales, Bernard asked, "What lesson can we gather from all this?" We didn't much care, the stories were so great in themselves. He went on to note that John Bosco had such a warm, attractive countenance and personality that the boys and adults (save the anticlericals) were naturally drawn to him. We shouldn't, Bernard exhorted in his delightful French-Canadian accent, have sourpusses. Amen to that, brother!

+

Today I taught the second class of my Camaldolese Constitutions course, for all the formation people. I am fairly charged up about it, and they seem interested too.

Part of Vatican II renewal was to require all Catholic religious orders to recast their basic documents, specifying how they intend to live their lives today. Such *Constitutions* are juridical documents that set out how a congregation is to be governed, how formation works, what the vows are, etcetera. In our drafting committees after the Council, we quickly came to the conclusion that we could spell out these juridical points only in the light of our fundamental theology and spirituality.

Thus, our *Constitutions* are interwoven with what we call our *Declarations,* which set forth the principles of faith and practice that determine the juridical points. Rome was not too excited about the spirituality stuff, they simply wanted the juridical; but we stressed that for us they are inseparable, so Rome allowed us to keep them together on condition that we distinguish them typographically. We put the theology and spirituality in **bold type,** the other in light.

We have a rather bold first paragraph to get the whole thing going:

> Long before the coming of Christ, humanity's quest for the Absolute gave rise in various religious traditions to expressions of monastic life. The many different forms of monastic and ascetical life bear witness to the divine destiny of the human person and to the presence of the Spirit in the hearts of all who seek to know what is true and ultimately real. [58]

Fr. Thomas Matus had these ideas in mind and expressed how truly universal the monastic life is, when in 1985 he wrote a fascinating pamphlet for distribution to guests and visitors at the Hermitage.

> There is something of the monk in every person, a kind of universal monastic archetype. To understand monasticism it is necessary to get in touch with this archetype, the monk within. And this is just as necessary for someone who has spent years living in a monastery as it is for the person who is approaching monasticism for the first time.
>
> Monastics—monks and nuns—are called to manifest the universal archetype and to realize it concretely, not for themselves only but for all humanity. Responding to this vocation, they experience the benevolence and compassion which the hidden God pours out upon all creatures. As they grow in the monastic way, they learn to show compassion to others, without making distinctions and without passing judgment. And they know that they are never alone, even though they may dwell in the desert, far from human society. [59]

Being alone is often looked upon as an aberration. Certain monastics embrace the state, not as an anti-social perversion, but, in part, as a continuation of a very long history indeed. Matus continues:

> The earliest monastic figures are from India. One is the naked wanderer of the *Rig Veda*. Free as the wind, he is a symbol of the demand for transcendence, the basic human need to move beyond the limits of what heredity and environment have made us.
>
> Another early monastic figure is Siddhartha Gautama, The Buddha. His story was transformed into a Christian legend around the end of the seventh century. Which simply means that the Buddha's story is also archetypal and can evoke the monastic in monks and in everyone.[60]

These texts and that first paragraph of the *Constitutions* explicitly note the incredible diversity of forms of monasticism down through the ages. 'Unity in diversity' is one of our mottos, and we did not just come up with it by ourselves. The richly varied world history of monasticism requires it.

+

Many contemporary Americans often suffer from a sense of rootlessness, of being cut off from any significant past. Others are not even aware of this alienation in their lives. Yet others flaunt their disdain for the past: "History is bunk!" proclaimed Henry Ford. (If history is mainly about producing and selling automobiles, there isn't much to learn from anything before our century. But if there is more to history and to us than that...)

Our *Constitutions* trace, from the first page of the Introduction, a monastic heritage that predates Christianity, and then finds its Christian basis in Scripture, and primarily in Christ. In the *Constitutions* this is followed by reference to the 'early Church ascetics and virgins,' then to 'the earliest monks of the third and the fourth centuries, with the exodus to the desert.' Then we have St. Benedict, St. Romuald, and the whole procession of Christian nuns and monks to our own time. All this is to say that our own life here has not been improvised, 'dreamed up' by some committee. It is the living twig of a branch of a tree that is deeply rooted in the dark soil of prehistory. We are

in communion with centuries of monastics down through the ages—and mysteriously with all those who will come after us until the end of the world. Monastics should have some idea of who they are and where they are going, given that they have an idea of from whom and whence they have come.

When I was in Italy during the lively 1960s and 1970s, I did some research on Utopian communities. There has been a great variety in Europe and the U.S. since the beginning of the last century, based on every kind of ideology. But however brilliant their founders, and however generous their members, they rarely survived into a second generation. Our monastery in Rome goes back to Pope Gregory the Great and the sixth century. Our Sacred Hermitage in Tuscany goes back to the early eleventh century. Our monastery of Fonte Avellana recently celebrated its thousandth year (with a helicopter visit from the Pope and the issuing of a special postage stamp!) This place, even this place in California could well survive until the end of time, simply because the heritage is so rich, the lineage so unbroken, the values so perennial.

Another way to put it (hopefully without excessive pride of place) is: If someone is male and Catholic, is prepared for celibacy and feels drawn to contemplative union with God, then the Hermitage is not a bad place to be. It is not the only place available—one of the great virtues of the Catholic Church is that it offers a range of contemplative communities—but this particular mountainside is comparable to the others. And our principal ministry is to affirm and support this same contemplative yearning in everyone, through our guest ministry, our network of oblates and friends, our writing and other outreach.

+

A young Dominican just made his Solemn Profession retreat with us. He left us a gracious thank-you note, with a very profound and Thomist thought from the 'Master of the Dominican Order:'

> We cannot be alone
> because alone we could not even be!
> TIMOTHY RADCLIFFE, O.P.

If we get beyond a wooly deism, according to which God the Watchmaker put us together, wound us up and set us off on our own; if we realize that only God is necessary Existence, and our very contingent, fragile being is constantly coming forth and being sustained by that Existence, as a sung note comes forth and is sustained by a singer; if we can somehow come to terms with all this, then we can begin to appreciate the good Dominican Master's insight.

+

Camaldolese are simply monks, part of the monastic heritage. We do not have a founder as the Franciscans have in St. Francis, or the Jesuits in St. Ignatius. We do follow the *Rule of St. Benedict,* and we are members of the Benedictine Confederation, and St. Romuald's medieval reform was decisive for our own Camaldolese reform. But we are still simply monks, and if we visit an Eastern monastery, we do not announce ourselves as Benedictines or Camaldolese, but as monks of the Western Church. Eastern Monks do not think of themselves as Basilians, if they should happen to follow St. Basil's Rule, but rather as monks of the Eastern Church. Is this just a question of semantics? Maybe not.

But having said that we are simply monks, and not 'Benedictines' or 'Romualdians,' it remains true that we are profoundly influenced by St. Benedict's Rule and St. Romuald's later reform. The two saints are similar in many respects—their single-minded search for God, their sense of discretion, their human compassion. But they are different in others: Benedict was a legislator, and liked order. Romuald was charismatic, and was constantly up to new and surprising things as the Spirit moved him. Benedict allowed an opening to solitude, and had high esteem for authentic anchorites,[61] but he wrote primarily for cenobites, 'the strong kind of monks.'[62] Romuald, on the other hand, began in a cenobitic abbey, and indeed sometimes returned to community. But his heart was clearly for the solitary life, and he lived mostly in solitude. Benedict especially esteemed liturgy as the monk's expression of prayer. Romuald seems to have favored the solitary recitation of Psalms and silent prayer in the Spirit. Whereas Benedict stressed cloistered stability, Romuald was often on the move. We Camaldolese are somewhere between these creative poles, as most monks are in some way or other, because the same dialectic is already found in the Egyptian desert in the first part of the fourth century, embodied in the monks Anthony and Pachomius. Indeed, the juxtaposition is already found in Scripture, in the play between the Law and the Prophets, and in the intense life of Jesus, who, announcing that he came not to abolish the Law but to fulfill it,[63] immediately moved beyond the Law, teaching: 'You have heard that it was said...but I say to you...'[64]

+

In terms of the Benedict-Romuald dialectic, we can set up a schema of four polarities, albeit facile, oversimplified:

Institution	—	Charism
Community	—	Solitude
Liturgy	—	Prayer in Silence
Stability	—	Dynamism

During my Constitutions class I put this up on the board and Isaiah whimsically suggested that it might serve as our own, specialist version of the Myers-Briggs lists. He suggested that he, for instance, would be more *I*nstitutional, more for *S*olitude, more *L*iturgical, more for *S*tability. So we could give him the letters ISLS. As for me, I would be planted roughly in the middle of the polarities, in my heart of hearts tending towards a CCPS. And so each monk might evaluate himself (and make himself open to fraternal feedback). If this were to become anywhere near as big as Myers-Briggs, there could be major money to be made!

+

Maurice Blondel, the great Catholic philosopher and theologian, suggested that in its institution-charism dialectic, Christianity is like a great volcano. Every now and then there is a mighty eruption and the fiery lava explodes up and out. But then it runs down the mountain, cools, forms hardened channels, builds up the mountain. In time another explosion follows and the cycle begins again.

February 2nd
The Presentation

Just before Vigils we gathered at the ikon of Mary and Child and blessed the candles. Gabriel had turned the lights down so everything was quite dark, and he had piled boxes and boxes of candles in front of the ikon, and laid out on top of the cartons samples of the candles that were receiving the transforming benediction: big candles, small candles, medium-sized candles. *Che bello!* Devotion is alive at New Camaldoli.

Someone started handing out unlit tapers. Someone else said no, first the blessing, so the tapers were returned to their little table (our Master of Ceremonies, Matthew, is away at Incarnation Monastery for his spiritual direction course). I could hardly see the prayers, even with my glasses off and squinting. Hopefully my sacerdotal-presidential dignity was not excessively diminished. After I blessed and sprinkled holy water, we passed out the tapers again, two of us lit ours from the paschal candle which Joshua adeptly proffered, then we spread the flame to others, they to others, and in a very brief time everyone had a lit candle, (one could get a sermon out of that!) Then we processed into the chapel, singing the Hymn of the Presentation. All this is just a slight addition to our usual Vigils liturgy, we did it last year too. It makes a lovely difference to the day, and serves to distinguish the celebration.

+

In the morning I called the Diocesan office in Fairbanks, Alaska, to talk with the Chancellor again about our property in Ruby. She was out, but the secretary enthusiastically said, "Oh do come up! We so need priests!" Actually, that isn't quite the right thing to say to a monk. If we were to send up monks, they would be monks first, and any priest of their number would need to be very wary of parish or mission service.

In the late afternoon Bro. Kirby returned the call. He had been seconded by the Chancellor. That makes sense, because he knows Ruby like the back of his gloves. That is his base, though as Coordinator of Native Alaskan Ministries, he journeys all over the diocese. I asked him about the weather—20°F below! There are only two hours of sunlight a day at the moment, I think, I didn't get it clearly... But it was his dime and I had to get to the question: how he viewed the prospect of monks in Ruby. He was very courteous and noted that he had some experience with monasteries, being a native Kentuckian and having visited Gethsemani Abbey. He was not sure that our main ministries—retreats and hospitality—would work well, simply because the place is so remote, usually only accessible by plane. The little town has a solid Catholic community, shepherded by three women. A priest comes only twice a month. It is the ladies who conduct the regular communion services (what would Msgr. Lefebvre have to say about that!) The delicate implication of our conversation was, it seemed to me, that the establishment of a contemplative monastery in such a little place, with daily liturgies carried out by Anglos, might be something of an imposition upon the delicate rhythm of local Native Alaskan Church life. I don't know whether or not Bro. Kirby intended to imply this. It is a question I will have to raise later.

FEBRUARY 3RD
SAINTS ANSGAR AND BLASE

At Saturday Chapter I tried to bring the brethren into the loop regarding the possibility of the Arizona house of prayer becoming ours. The Franciscan sister who for years has been the Director, is getting on a bit, and indicated to Cyprian during his visit last month that she would look positively upon our having it after her retirement. The property belongs to the diocese, but she told Cyprian that 'Bishop Tom,' who had made a retreat there recently, expressed concern over what would happen when the sister retired, and would possibly favor us taking over the establishment. That is all to be seen. The book *Sanctuaries: The West Coast and Southwest* offers this little picture:

> Up a long, steep drive to a mesa in the Sonoran Desert, this house-of-prayer complex sits alone and quiet. It's hard to imagine a more fitting place for solitude and contemplative prayer. [65]

We are so crowded here, and there being some eight tentative candidates in this upcoming postulancy group puts pressure on us to explore further foundations. This place in Arizona could be a small hermitage with a guest house, or a small cenobium with guest hermitages—or we could mix it up a bit, with our monks usually in the little cenobium, but with periods in the hermitages when they are empty—that sort of thing. The *Sanctuaries* book gives this description of the main house, which we think might serve as a little guest house or cenobium:

> At the end of the drive, the main house sits on a high point with sweeping desert views to the south and west. There are six private guest rooms with shared baths in the house, which has a spacious reading room stocked with more than 1,400 books; meals are taken in the adjacent dining room.[66]

Then the authors offer this description of the freestanding chapel:

> On a separate knoll is the Dwelling Place, a chapel dedicated in 1988. The circular stucco building has a picture window looking out over the valley below; a window-cross of stained glass depicting Christ in a collage of color is the only decoration in the subdued interior.[67]

And regarding the cells:

> Near the chapel are four sturdy and comfortable hermitages set apart from one another. Each hermitage has a kitchenette, a single bedroom, a private bath, and cooling and heating units. The absolute privacy enables retreatants to appreciate the silence and sweetness of the surrounding desert air.[68]

I talked with Sr. Therese by phone a couple of days ago, and she reiterated what she had told Cyprian, and in very gracious terms. I immediately sent her a package of our booklets, postcards, and newsletters, and she sent some material to us which I pinned on our bulletin board: her lovely note, a postcard and a little folder. I put more reading matter and some maps of Arizona on the library table. So, there was some background information for today's discussion among the brethren.

Basically, we are in favor of writing to the Bishop—which Sr. Therese suggests—to indicate our real interest in exploring the possibilities. Unfortunately, the location—45 minutes to the north of Phoenix— means that such a foundation would not be within easy reach of here or of Incarnation. Our dream would be to have a place between these two houses. But at least the site is much more accessible than Epiphany, way out in New Hampshire.

At the same Chapter we discussed Ruby, Alaska, in the light of Bro. Kirby's phone-call. I do not think that we have closed the door on a possible monastic presence there, but it is a long-shot. Arizona appears more likely.

The challenge of being crowded here is sometimes eased in a less happy way—by men moving on to something else. Sometimes it is the community that concludes that things are not working out; sometimes it is the individual; sometimes it is a consensus.

Certainly we are not the only act in town. There are all kinds of ways to serve the Lord in this big world. Still and all, there is always some grieving on both sides—and often a great deal— when a man leaves. And inevitably we who remain ask ourselves (as we should) if we might not have done more to facilitate the man's continuing here.

Some who go on leave return—and that is a cause of real joy. And of those who do not, we are relieved that the great majority maintain a bond of friendship with us. They say that their time with us has been valuable to them, and such men have contributed a great deal to our life while they were here, and their friendship continues to enrich us. So we thank God for our 'alumni,' and pray for their ongoing journey in the Lord. And we are comforted by the faith that in the Kingdom we will all be one forever and ever

+

I presided at Mass today, and said at the Greeting that it would be an action-packed Eucharist. Bruno beamed at that. I like it when he beams. I explained that we were celebrating the great ninth-century monastic Archbishop St. Ansgar, and also the mysterious martyr Blase, who is so effective against midwinter throat maladies. And we were also celebrating the reception of an oblate. Our oblate family is growing steadily.

+

The first reading today had to do with the young Solomon de-voutly worshipping God on the mountaintop, offering a thousand holocausts. God is so moved he offers Solomon whatever he asks. Solomon prays for an understanding heart, and the capacity to distinguish right from wrong. God is delighted that Solomon does not ask for wealth or long life or vengeance against enemies. [69] And all this is in immediate preparation for building the Temple.

All very moving, but how do we claim such a text for ourselves today? —Or rather, how do we permit it to claim us? I mentioned in my homily that a fundamentalist application would relate Solomon to sovereigns of our own time. In anglophile mode, I noted that Queen Elizabeth II certainly has an understanding heart, though she need not build a temple with St. Paul's Cathedral already on the Thames. An extended application, I argued, would be to all national leaders, all people in power. Do they seek power, glory, vengeance? Or do they seek an understanding heart to serve their people? Here the Word of God empowers us to a prophetic stance toward authority figures. All well and good, but does the text actually challenge *us* in this approach?

Then I mentioned the classic approach of the early and later Fathers and Mothers, and the medieval monastic exegetes, an approach they find already in St. Paul and the Gospels and throughout the New Testament: that is, a 'christological' reading. What does the Solomon text reveal about Christ? This apparently odd approach is based on the faith conviction that there is a providential unfolding to salvation history, and this is expressed in a providential unfolding of Scripture. Moses and David and Solomon are preparing for Christ—whether they know it or not, whether the redactors of the passages about them know it or not (and clearly, *not* is the case).

So, in our Solomon passage today, he is the son of David— in preparation for *the* Son of David. He offers his sacrifice on the mountaintop, as does Christ, always, in the 'apex of his spirit.' He asks for a wise heart, and Christ has that, which, when pierced, nourishes us all. Solomon builds the Temple; and Christ's body *is* the Temple:

'Destroy this temple, and in three days I will raise it up.'
...But he spoke of the temple of his body. [70]

If the text is about Christ, it is about us. We are 'made Christ,' as St. Augustine affirms. As we share in his priesthood and prophetic ministry, we share his regal nature. And in fact each of us is a little realm, with all kinds of villages and towns within, with whole populations of personages, roles, emotions, scattered here and there. Our ongoing dreams reveal something of the inner kingdom, as do our various social personalities. The Solomon text invites us to preside, under the kingship of Christ, over this mysterious interior realm, avoiding anarchy on the one extreme, and tyranny on the other.

We do not have to build the temple, only acknowledge that Christ has come in the flesh, that He is the Temple. And so too are *we*, according to this Pauline shift from the christological to the inclusive:

> Do you not know that your body is a temple of the Holy Spirit? [71]

Thus the Solomon passage invites us to revere the Temple by becoming truly incarnate, and worship in the Temple by opening to the Spirit.

+

The Bishop of Fairbanks phoned today, recommending a local Ruby family as possible purchasers of our property there. Very honest, he says, generous church people. So we held a quick Chapter after Eucharist, and voted ten-to-zero to move forward with the negotiations. It was only a 'Mind of the Chapter' vote, with some absent capitulars completely unaware of the new situation. I have been in touch with them all this afternoon, through voice mail and letter, asking their thoughts. Then we will have an official vote on Thursday morning.

FEBRUARY 4TH

I am sometimes struck by the thought that if I had to do it all over again, I would. This monastic life. And knowing what I know, I would have a much better time. I think nowadays our formation program is deeper and more solid that when I entered, and I could avoid some pitfalls that surprised me first time around.

Then I reflect that I would go to the same college again. Pomona offered a very good liberal arts education. I could well choose another college or university, but in any event, I would enjoy a second chance. I would focus less on the grade-point average and snowing the professor, and more on getting into the substance of the materials in order to retain them long-term— not just until five minutes after the exam. I would be more aware of others, of things happening among students and professors.

My mom used to say that she would never want to have to live her teens over again. But I would not mind, or the pre-teens either. Does this mean I have missed something of the darkness of all these stages? Am I too much of a Pollyanna?

Then, to sober me up, I have to realize that there is the future, Though perhaps not too much of it. In a sense, I have to go through a new postulancy, novitiate and period of temporary vows, in preparation for the final vows of death—and resurrection. This is the really big formation program. I find myself as a freshman, a beginner again, not quite sure how it is done. Christ and the Gospels certainly help.

Then there is the present. And it is all here. Novitiate and Pomona and high school and the crib. And also final sickness and death. And resurrection.

+

I had a good conversation this afternoon with a young man who has left the Catholic Church and who tentatively identifies himself with the Assemblies of God. He is studying in one of their colleges, into his fourth year. This is his second retreat here. His early Catholic years had been dominated by fear of ecclesial authority, rules and condemnations, and the fierce God behind them. When he explored the reform tradition, he experienced the saving love of Jesus there. The Scriptures suddenly became truly Good News for him. Jesus was—and is—experienced as the living Lord.

All that Catholic stuff is still inside him, and renewed through Vatican II. Even in his college he is being assigned books by Catholics—in Scripture and spirituality. And he is starting to experience liturgy in a new way—not as a flat, almost magical rite of the priests to be observed from a distance, but as worship of the community of faith. He is particularly drawn to the praying of the Psalms and the fact that we monks are so at home with them, and that we recite them in a way that is not just a proclamation by one reader, but prayer of the whole community.

He had several questions about praying the Psalms—what about the malediction verses? How does one follow all the ideas and emotions? I have loved the Psalms since early in my teens when I was an Anglican, and was able to say some things from experience. I was moved by the man's deep living faith and commitment. In our language, he is a contemplative and a mystic.

I was careful not to indulge in proselytism. Nor was he remotely preaching the Assemblies of God to me. In the end we both rejoiced in being called to be 'bridge people,' and committed ourselves to pray for each other. It was a wonderful moment of grace.

+

Today at the Sunday lunch table there were the Assemblies of God chap, then two women priests of the Episcopal Church, both good friends from years ago, and two of the younger brethren, John and Raniero, both of them very ecumenical and very sharp. We had a delightful exchange about the different denominations, various ways of worship, therapy and religion, and models of God.

February 17th

I have a new computer and *Windows 95*, thanks to much help from James. My head is spinning. I feel like an aborigine who suddenly finds himself walking down Fifth Avenue in New York. How do this astonishing machine and the vistas it opens relate to monastic and contemplative life? Some would see absolute opposition. Our life is concerned with moving into the poverty and silence of the heart and surrendering to God. The computer is the means to moving out onto the Web and accessing and controlling more and more trivial information—distraction in the most literal sense. Taken more humbly, the computer does facilitate the editing of a text—to the relief of writer and reader. And some of the forums which one encounters on the Web are about contemplative prayer, Thomas Merton, the Church today, and so on. Perhaps I had better neither demonize nor worship it.

Today in Saturday Chapter I talked about the Abbots/Priors Workshop, and especially about the twelve conferences given by Fr. Paul Philibert on Celibacy. At the end he had joked that the invitation to speak had forced him to think more in a few months about this topic than he had in a lifetime. Later, one abbot, on the way to the airport, humphed that perhaps that was the problem: he had spent all the time *thinking* about something that was not to be borne just intellectually. But I think that Fr. Paul, without getting too cerebral (though he is, after all, a Dominican) provided us with some very substantial theology. Some would have put forth a more casuistic approach: what we should do in such-and-such a disordered case. Rather, it seems to me, he gave the underpinnings for the pastoral response to any case.

FEBRUARY 18TH
SIXTH SUNDAY OF THE YEAR

A Latino choir of about twenty persons of all ages, drove three hours to be with us for Eucharist, and shook the walls with their wonderful singing. It was quite a contrast between our sober Anglo-monastic liturgy and the exuberant, festive Latino celebration. Afterwards, before the Marian ikon, they sung hymn after hymn to Our Lady. I was moved by their deep, simple faith. Catholicism at its best!

FEBRUARY 21ST
ASH WEDNESDAY

W e had a rough ceramic bowl filled with ashes at the center of the choir all day today, to remind us of Ash Wednesday, the beginning of Lent. Bruno preached about ashes and the striking symbol of signing the forehead with them. It is appropriate to do so because ashes represent the Earth. Modern man (sexist language intended) is a huge head supported by two spindly legs. To sign the head with the earth is to reaffirm a desperately needed conjunction. And to be truly in touch with the Earth again, Bruno went on, we need to be in touch with the people of the Earth, the *Anawim,* the Native Americans, and people of the Third World. Thus, there is a prophetic thrust to Lent.

But the ashes more specifically indicate a tree, a burned tree. It reminds us of that first tree in the Garden, which got us into so much trouble, a burned tree that calls out to the other Tree, the Cross which connects Earth to Heaven. So, the old Adam and the false self call out to the true self, the New Adam, Christ.

+

I received a long fax from Ezekiel, our student in Rome. His first semester grades are splendid, and he is now thinking of focusing on Scripture studies after the theology course. I am encouraging him as much as I can, and in replying I quoted from Vatican II (it is important to be as erudite as possible with these young 'uns!) to the effect that Scripture is 'the primary and perpetual foundation of theology, and its soul,' [DEI VERBUM, 24].

There was also a fax from Zacchaeus at his seminary, John XXIII, near Boston. His second semester classes seem to be more intense than before. But he is doing well, among other things studying Sign Language for his future pastoral work.

Then there was an e-mail from another of our students, Randy, in Berkeley. He is off to San Francisco General Hospital to work with AIDS victims, as part of his Clinical Pastoral Education. It is exciting having these gifted young men preparing in such varied ways for their future life with us.

FEBRUARY 22ND
THE CHAIR OF ST. PETER

B runo whimsically refers to this feast as being about ecclesiastical furniture. Louis grumbled about the feast a bit in the sacristy when we twitted him for not having on a solemn stole for the Mass. He murmured, "All these churchy feasts! It is as if the Church sometimes wants to worship itself!" I gave the homily and, without naming names, referred to both these comments, which drew some smiles. I noted that this is a very ancient feast, going back to the fourth century, and its intent is to honor the ministry and primacy of Peter among the Apostles, and the ministries of his successors among the bishops. If only from a purely historical perspective, the papacy is astonishing in its antiquity and its continuity. Is there anything quite like it in the West—or the East? Some find a comparison with the Dalai Lama, but that only underlines how unique the papacy is. Certainly the present Dalai Lama is a profound spiritual leader, but in terms of antiquity of lineage, he is the fourteenth Dalai Lama, whereas John Paul II is the two hundred and sixty-fourth Pope. The office of Dalai Lama began in the fifteenth century when the papacy was already ancient. How many emperors and empires, rulers and regimes have come and gone, and yet the papacy endures? And in some ways it is more influential than ever. Now there are hundreds of millions of Catholics, and John Paul II is in some sense the shepherd of that flock, however restless it may be. I remember an Anglican professor at the Episcopal School in Berkeley insisting that only Christ is our Shepherd, that all the rest of us, however high on the ecclesiastical ladder, are not shepherds but sheepdogs at most, with the task of keeping the flock gathered and protected and following the Shepherd. It is a delightful image: John Paul II, Sheepdog of Our Souls! Some feel he nips at the heels a bit too much.

It is remarkable that the first thirty-five popes are saints, many of them martyrs. As I went through the list of pontiffs, I found seventy-eight saints in all, including some true giants: Gregory the Great and Leo the Great, for instance. For many of us John XXIII, of our own time, is a saint and giant. It is salutary to visit his tomb in the crypt of the Vatican and witness all the faithful praying there, the banks of flowers. Other nearby tombs are less frequented.

For a Camaldolese monk, the constant affirmation of the contemplative vocation by the successors of Peter is striking and reassuring. In his 1982 visit to our ancient monastery at Fonte Avellana in Italy, the Pope gave this address:

> I want to express to you my great gratitude for your life of prayer and study, and for your ministry on behalf of the Church… The first thought that comes to me is to invite all to value as much as possible silence and contemplation. In this place such a consideration is taken for granted. But it is most important to repeat this, especially today with the ever faster pace of events, the frenetic rush of activities of modern life. Your monastery reaffirms the essential value of the in-

terior life, of union with God... It is precisely in our own
time that this aspiration is more pressing...And so monastic
life maintains its full value in the contemporary world, and
is witness and encouragement to society in general... I have
come to drink of the fountain of spirituality, in this
atmosphere where everything witnesses to the values of the
Spirit. Here where silence reigns and peace prevails, God
speaks to our hearts. I greet with sincere affection the
Camaldolese community... You choose to dwell in silence
and solitude, so as to open yourselves more fully to the
mystery of God. Thus doing you put yourselves in direct
contact with Christ, and occupy an eminent place in the
Church... In fact, Camaldolese spirituality today, in virtue
of the wonderful renewal received from Vatican II, is more
flourishing than ever in the Church, and constitutes a great
source of grace and spiritual help for all Christians, indeed
for all of humanity... Allow me to offer you the exhortation
to love ever more your life. [73]

Helpful exhortation, as so many of his are. Too bad, the less
affirming, more punitive themes in the Vatican's messages to others.

FEBRUARY 23RD
SAINT POLYCARP

B runo said in his homily that this great second-century martyr was burned at the stake, and the contemporaneous lyrical account of his martyrdom speaks of St. Polycarp as being
gold refined in the fire, eucharistic bread baked in the oven. It
seems to me that we have our little daily fires which could serve
the same transformative purpose were we rightly to claim the
off-putting experiences. Bruno commented that we can still see
the light of Polycarp's immolation, down through the centuries, and it can still illuminate our lives if we let it. He noted
that there are other fires, alas, in our history, like the fires of
the Inquisition, which cast a long dark shadow down to our time.
These two very different kinds of fire are like the two kinds of
zeal St. Benedict speaks of in chapter 72 of the *Rule:*

> Just as there is a wicked zeal of bitterness which separates
> from God and leads to hell, so there is a good zeal which
> separates from evil and leads to God and everlasting life.

So, there are two kinds of religion, that of the Grand Inquisitor, and that of the gentle Bishop Polycarp. And the dance goes on!

+

Today I phoned my very good friend, Suzanne Guthrie. She is an Episcopal priest, author, mother, wife—she fulfills several ministries with real grace. Appropriately, her new book is entitled *Grace's Window: Entering the Seasons of Prayer.* It includes a wonderful blurb on the back cover (by me!)

> These pages achieve an astonishing conjunction of real, hard life with Christian contemplation. Suzanne Guthrie's love of family, church and humanity comes to wonderful fruition in these meditations on prayer.

That is the task proposed to each of us daily.

Suzanne and I first met years ago in Berkeley at the Graduate Theological Union. We presented conferences together on the English Mystics. At a rollicking party to conclude the thing, I rushed around with a sheet over me (representing the Cloud of Unknowing) and she was Julian of Norwich (or was it Richard Rolle?) We dramatized to the startled audience the spiritual encounter of these towering mystics. Since then we have held all sorts of conferences and retreats together. I am the godfather of her brilliant youngest son, Patrick, (now, alas in public school, not in a good parochial school as he ought to be).

My call today was in response to her message: she would be in Berkeley soon, and so will I. Unfortunately we will miss each other by a day. She told me of a dream she had just had. It involved me and her in a convent. I was blown up, killed, immediately canonized, etcetera. She really should talk more with a good therapist!

February 24th

S aturday Chapter. I continued to explore the theme of classic celibacy with the brethren, in the light of the conferences of Fr. Paul Philibert. If we take the immensity of the eros drive at all seriously, as well as our wounded condition, the call to some kind of chaste Christian life is an immense challenge. It is not something I resolved once and for all years ago with monastic (or marriage) vows. Rather it is a kind of moment-by-moment adventure, especially if, as Philbert said, authentic celibacy is not about saying *No* to love, but rather shouting *Yes!* to unconditional Love, and all in Love.

Philbert used some insights of Freud (about sublimation) so I provided the brethren with a splendid blackboard diagram of the human psyche according to elemental Freudianism (the *Cliff Notes* version), with the SUPEREGO above, and a big arrow thrusting down from it, the ID below, with a big arrow thrusting up from it, and the poor ego caught in the middle, trying to mediate these two ferocious counter-forces, and deal at the same time with 'reality out there.' Then I added to the board the distinctly non-Freudian dimension of GOD 'behind' the ego.

Celibacy can seem like a total capitulation to the superego, which is shouting 'No, No! Dirty!' at the intimidated ego, who accepts the threats and turns around and desperately represses the Id. But in Philbert's presentation (as well as in any healthy understanding of celibacy and chaste married life), the Christian acknowledges the full force and legitimacy of the erotic drives and all the other intense stuff of the Id—anger, fear, etcetera—and seeks with the grace of God to direct all this toward the Mystery where it can be handled and interpreted. The superego at its best can hardly object to this.

The basic Freudian schema can tell us quite a lot about the individual, and about communities, also churches, states, political campaigns (we are in the middle of a wild one) and so on. Regarding the superego, there does seem to be a vital energy inside us that has internalized the prohibitions of our parents, teachers and society, and it is constantly trying to keep us on the straight and narrow. And, in real tension with that, there

is a wild beast within each of us, urging us to cut loose. And it is at the community level that this dynamic continues, though in a civil mode! Some people have more regard for law and order, for going by the book, while others want to act spontaneously, and for things to open up. I moralized that hopefully in a healthy, mature community we are all trying to acknowledge both creative poles, rather than dividing and polarizing: one group specializing in the control agenda and others concentrating on the let's-have-some-fun proposal. (I am currently miffed at one of the brethren who frequently plays the subversive Dionysian, to the astonishment of the more devout!)

Even in this simplified form, the Freudian model offers insight into Church dynamics—certainly things Roman Catholic. Has the superego co-opted central (and subordinate) authority, and are the laity being pushed, by reaction, more and more in the opposite direction? At least many perceive that Rome is becoming more and more truculent: the sad photograph of the Pope frowning and pointing his finger at a kneeling Fr. Ernesto Cardenal during that dramatic papal trip to Nicaragua, springs to mind.

And what about current U.S. politics? For many of us, a Pat Buchanan type can represent the angry superego, taking over, building walls, excluding those dangerous foreigners. 'Law and Order' is again ascendant, though others would insist that lawless hedonism still prevails.

Several of the brethren participated in the lively discussion. David argued that these basic insights are already in Scripture, indeed in the Jewish Scriptures (and Freud was a Jew!) Is not the biblical 'fear' equivalent to the effects of the superego? And does not the biblical category 'flesh' correspond to the agenda of the Id? It seems to me he is right.

Louis, who is studying for a Master's degree in psychology, pointed out that there is not just the interior play of subjective forces, but that outside reality impinges upon the psyche at every moment. I agreed, noting that the ego is supposed to move ahead, according to the 'reality principle' in order to counter the Id's 'pleasure principle.' Michael, back from his Graduate Theological Union studies, made an analogous comment, but from the point of view of the subject: that reason can guide a person safely, and help articulate a personal, conscious sense of morality that is free from the oppression of the superego. Bruno said that the Freudian model seems irreducibly, pessimistically conflictive. Is there not some deeper subjective center beyond ego, which is definitely not simply Id or superego? I agreed: here the more optimistic Jungian model is more consonant with the Christian anthropology. There is a *self* that opens the way to the Ultimate, that yearns for the Ultimate. Hence the *Spirit* in the Pauline letters and the Fathers.

+

I once heard a man say about becoming sober: 'I was given permission to be ordinary.' What a relief! Not to be better than or less than, to be special only as part of. What is special is to be ordinary.

CAROL BUCKLEY, *AT THE STILL POINT—A MEMOIR*

+

Prayer is a supreme good. It is a partnership and union with God. As the eyes of the body are enlightened when they see light, so our spirit when it is intent on God, is illumined by his infinite light. I do not mean the prayer of outward observance, but prayer from the heart, not confined to fixed times or periods, but continuous throughout the day or night. Our spirit should be quick to reach out toward God, not only when it is engaged in meditation, but at other times also; when it is carrying out its duties, caring for the needy, performing works of charity, giving generously in the service of others. Our spirit should long for God, so that these works may be seasoned with the salt of God's love, and so make a palatable offering to the Lord of the Universe. Throughout the whole of our lives we may enjoy the benefit that comes from prayer if we devote a great deal of time to it. Prayer is the light of the spirit. The spirit, raised up to heaven by prayer, clings to God with the utmost tenderness, like a child crying tearfully for its mother, it craves the milk that God provides.[74]

ST. JOHN CHRYSOSTOM

FEBRUARY 26TH

A ndrew, Prior of our little Berkeley community, is in Chicago, ministering to the Italian-American community, so Incarnation is without a priest. I drive up today to fill in for about a week. Highway 1 from the Hermitage winds along the coast for some glorious views of ocean and mountains. But then I cross over to Highway 101 and sprawling megalopolis begins: billboards and noise of every sort. It is a culture shock at first, but I adapt—too easily?

Our Berkeley house is fortunately a little above the city, and is surrounded by trees and adjacent to a little park, giving the immediate context something of a rural feel. Below, the whole Bay Area extends—another glorious view, though unlike Big Sur! To take full advantage of the view there are glass doors and numerous windows, and each of the three floors has a deck running the length of the Bay side.

Our three Incarnation monks greet me. Then we have a long-term guest, Robert, a Hawaiian of Japanese background. He is working on his doctorate about how political conditions affect the life of Asian religions.

Randy and Gregory are studying at the Graduate Theological Union. So Incarnation also functions as our house of studies, and the liturgical life and workload are slimmed down to facilitate this. The school assignments are extremely heavy. We maintain that our monks are monks first, not academics, but all things considered, studies are important if our men are going to be well prepared for their prayer and ministry.

We prayed Vespers after I arrived. It is a much more sober liturgy than at New Camaldoli where we sing all the hymns, psalms, canticles and antiphons. Everything is recited here, and very slowly. At first this is disconcerting and guests (and visiting monks) tend to want to pick up the pace. But the Incarnation monks proceed in their own way, and others catch on. Very restful, a good antidote to the frenetic pace of the city.

FEBRUARY 28TH

L unch with Jan Baltz, one of our Berkeley oblates. An older woman, now single and retired, she has been a spiritual director for up to twenty-two people at a time. She reads constantly in spirituality, Scripture, theology and literature. And over her long life, and through so much spiritual direction she has heard it all. She is very rigorous about boundaries: does not direct friends, and does not like the direction relationship to become chummy. The Berkeley area can use boundaries!

FEBRUARY 29TH

R andy's studies include Clinical Pastoral Education. Every Wednesday he travels by subway or car to the San Francisco General Hospital to minister to men struggling with AIDS. One man died yesterday, Iban, from South America, just twenty-nine years old. His body was extremely emaciated and was connected to all kinds of tubes. The family had come from South America, the father gentle and compassionate, the mother angry. The caregivers prayed together to the last moment, and Randy had the distinct impression of the powerful, embracing presence of God.

MARCH 3RD
SUNDAY

T oday's Gospel related the Transfiguration: Jesus ascending a high mountain and becoming blindingly luminous. In my homily to the Incarnation community and friends, I talked about mountains. Every major religion has its sacred mountains. The Native Americans would often look to the mountains. Jungians speak of the mountain archetype, which means that within each of us, in our collective unconscious, there are sacred mountains. Certainly in Scripture there are many references to sacred mountains: Sinai, Carmel, the Mount of the Beatitudes, the Mount of the Ascension, etcetera. Two decisive mountains in Christian salvation history are the Mount of the Transfiguration (traditionally Mount Tabor), and the Mount of the Crucifixion (Mount Calvary). These two mountains are strictly related because the Transfiguration was intended to prepare and steel the Apostles for Christ's crucifixion—to prefigure Christ's final victory over death. It is Christ who confers on both mountains their significance, but on each he is present in different ways: on Tabor in blinding glory, on Calvary he is stripped, humiliated, executed. On both mountains Christ is shown between two men: on Tabor between Moses and Elijah, discussing as their Fulfillment, the Law and the Prophets. On Calvary he is between two crucified thieves, one cursing him, the other begging for forgiveness. Tabor is luminous in glory, Calvary shrouded in darkness. On Calvary God seems to be absent (viz. Christ's words of dereliction: 'My God, my God, why have you forsaken me?') On Tabor, God himself speaks, 'This is my beloved Son, hear Him.'

Both mountains are somehow inside each Christian (indeed, each human being) as the mystery of death and glory unfolds in every life. Tabor offers the wider horizon, from Calvary one can see only darkness and death. Yet from Tabor's summit, Calvary can be seen in the distance, and beyond Calvary, the Garden of the Resurrection and the Mount of Christ's Ascension.

The Calvary experience seems to prevail in our own dark, death-dominated century. But faith enables Tabor to be experienced as well. Moments of communion with friends, moments of reconciliation surely provide an experiential glimpse of the light of Tabor, as do moments of contemplative prayer, of deep communion with God. What are these things but an abiding in the light?

Two of the three Apostles with Jesus on Mount Tabor—Peter and James—appear to forget the experience of the light. Certainly, when they fled at Christ's arrest, they were fleeing the light of Tabor. But John, the beloved disciple, somehow hung in there, was able to stand even beneath the horrendous cross. There is something about love that facilitates remembering and enables us to hold on to lived experiences of God's glory, even through the difficult times. Some of the ancient Christian masters, so focused on the Taboric Light, stress that the real enemy is forgetfulness. The real faculty of remembering is love. When we hold on through love to the experience of Christ's light, we can persevere even through the darkest times. If we deny or forget that light we will be unable seriously to confront the darkness.

MARCH 7TH
SAINTS PERPETUA AND FELICITY

There was a Conventual Chapter today to consider the requests for final vows of three of our monks in simple (three-year) vows: Randy, Raniero and Benedict. Our older monks are at their very best in Chapter. This is a very solemn moment for we are deliberating about the life vocations of three men, their futures until death. The criteria are most unusual: we are not determining whether we *like* these guys, whether we approve of their political views or esthetic taste, or something like that. We are trying to determine whether God is calling them here until they die.

The three have already been here over five years: two months observership, one year postulancy, one year novitiate, three years in simple vows. They have a thorough knowledge of each of us and of the life here. After much pondering and prayer, they have each come to the conclusion, not that they like all of us, or agree with all of us about President Clinton, but each of them has become convinced that God is calling him to our life. How do we respond?

In the case of these three men, it was not too difficult. Even with a two-thirds majority required, they were all strongly affirmed.

The next step is the planning for the Profession liturgy on June 15th. The three are inviting some hundred and fifty people—family, friends, Zen Buddhist nuns, Native Americans. It is going to be something!

+

It is such folly to pass one's time fretting, instead of resting quietly in the heart of Jesus.

ST. THÉRÈSE OF LISIEUX

Raniero preached today on martyrdom. Regularly his Charismatic past bursts through and his homily catches fire. He mentioned that monasticism from the beginning was considered a kind of white martyrdom through the ongoing daily self-offering that celibate life requires. (And marriage? One wit has suggested it is a black-and-blue martyrdom!)

Then he said that our own Camaldolese heritage includes the yearning for martyrdom. That third 'good' of St. Bruno Boniface, after the goods of the cenobitic and the eremitic life: to go forth to evangelize the pagans, and very possibly to be martyred. Raniero did something original with this third 'good': he interiorized it. He suggested that all three goods are within every Camaldolese (and probably every monk, every Christian, every human being, we might add). The 'cenobitic' refers to the communal needs and ministries of each of us. The 'eremitical' acknowledges our yearning for deep solitude, to be with the Lord. But as we go into the heart, we discover dark, unrepentant, unconverted areas. And they emphatically resist the light of the Gospel. We need to die, to go into those areas, and those areas need to die, to be converted. Inner work, if it is rigorous, can indeed be martyrdom.

MARCH 9TH
ST. FRANCES OF ROME

In Saturday Chapter today, after announcements, we continued to explore the theme of chaste celibacy. Understood in its broadest meaning, such chastity challenges us at every moment. It is not just about avoiding sex and dirty thoughts. It is about adhering wholly, directly, simply, cleanly to God, and thus loving all creation in God. So, if I am narcissistically caught up in my own world, or too hooked on a project of mine, or clinging inappropriately to another, or to my own anger or fear—that too is lapsing into an unchaste heart. Celibacy is about the beatitude, 'Blessed are the poor of heart' which contains the astonishing promise, 'for they shall see God.'[75] Thus, Cassian makes 'purity of heart' the ongoing immediate goal of the monk.[76]

We briefly considered the various dimensions of chaste celibacy. First, the christological dimension—chaste celibacy as a radical self-giving to Christ, imitation of Christ, the paradigm of chaste celibacy. Then there is the ecclesial dimension: being freed by total oblation to love all in Christ, but with the 'love of benevolence' rather than concupiscence. Thirdly, there is the prophetic dimension: an emphatic 'No' to pansexualism— especially prophetic in our times which presuppose and even glorify the promiscuous. And finally there is the eschatological witness, a witness to The Kingdom where there will not be a giving in marriage, where mysteriously we shall be like the angels,[77] where, ecstatically, 'God shall be all in all.'[78]

With apologies to Erikson and the Whiteheads, we moved on to discuss some of the basic insights of Developmental Psychology. The fundamental, incontrovertible point of this school is that there are certain patterns of being and behavior which at one age might appear healthy, but which in another become at least inappropriate. There is a cartoon in a recent *New Yorker* which shows the solemn board meeting of some splendid corporation; one of the members raises his hand and asks, 'Can I go out to play now?' An edifying question from a nine year old, but surprising from a fifty-five year old executive. (Even though one might argue that such people should ask the question more often!) But human life is an unfolding, a development, and if we can identify the central tasks of each phase of life, this can be most helpful in developing maturity.

There are, according to the Developmental people, three central tasks that confront us throughout adulthood: identity, intimacy, and fruitfulness. These are neither mutually exclusive nor even sequential; rather, as I risk intimacy, I learn more about who I am, and become more fruitful. Fruitfulness illuminates who I am, and enables me to give myself to further intimacy.

We can wrestle with these moments in an atheistic frame of mind, (and often enough we all lapse into a *de facto* pragmatic atheism,) or try tackling the issues without reference to God. The atheistic is the dominant approach in our individualistic and secularist time, a time which engenders much psychological counseling and therapy. It is quite different to consider everything in the light of God. And if intimacy means intimacy with God, on God's terms, then this basic 'task' and opportunity has a unique character about it, and it leads directly into the contemplative and mystical life.

If fruitfulness is seen as being enabled not only by my achievements and gifts, but through the fecundity and grace of God, then adult maturity too has a distinctly spiritual and mystical and contemplative character. And seeing all in the light of God renders chastity (whether celibate or married) as a prerequisite for the life journey rather than a perfectionist ideal.

In the discussion, Bruno noted that Erickson's teaching on the development of the individual presupposes the family: the adult who has achieved fundamental personal identity, who then marries in primary intimacy, and who has children who express the adult's primary fecundity. I acknowledged that this is Erickson's model, but he also shows that celibates can attain a high level of intimacy and fruitfulness. The Whiteheads have developed this celibate unfolding of Erickson's teaching.[79] The challenge to the celibate is to discover in deep friendship the possibilities of real intimacy which in generous ministry forms an authentic fruitfulness in the Lord.

MARCH 10TH

A new observer is here, Robert Daniels. In putting his file in my cabinet, I came across an old file of my own, with some papers from the earliest years. Among these was my completed Preliminary Questionnaire for Prospective Postulants. I had filled it out in April 1959, when I was twenty-one. The concluding question was:

17. What attracts you to the eremitical life?

To which I had responded...

> Four reasons: first, because God is so supremely worthy of love, I want to love him supremely, directly and simply. I am very prone to distraction...solitude jolts me into recollection, which permits me to begin to love Him as He ought to be loved and as I wish to love Him. Secondly, I feel the need to travel to the heart of the Church to attain the fullness

of Christian existence: and though it is very presumptuous to undertake such a journey, the need is great. Third, I feel bound to offer myself to God, in behalf of my 'lost and beat generation' to make as direct and simple intercession as possible. Fourth, I simply feel and believe I am summoned to this life, and should I delay or refuse...I believe I would be much like the rich man who would sacrifice a great deal to follow Christ, but not everything.

Who *is* this zealous kid who is determined to stay in the fledgling Big Sur foundation until they throw him out, in order to love God? I am not entirely sure, but am moved by the re-encounter and want to recommit myself to his goals.

The reference to 'my lost and beat generation' sent me back to the writings of Ginsberg and Ferlighetti, to *A Coney Island of the Mind,* and to *Howl.* Some lines from the latter:

> I saw the best minds of my generation destroyed
> by madness,
> starving, hysterical, naked...
>
> who cowered in unshaven rooms in underwear,
> burning their money
> in wastebaskets and listening to the Terror through
> the wall,
> who got busted in their public beards returning
> through Laredo
> with a belt of marijuana for New York,
> who ate fire in painted hotels or drank turpentine
> in Paradise Alley,
> death, or purgatoried their torsos, night after night,
> with dreams, with drugs, with waking nightmares,
> alcohol... [80]

Such a generation wants some prayers, it still seems to me.

In my application folder there was a copy of my reply to a letter from Jack Miller, the Pomona College professor of physics. He had written to me as soon as he heard I intended to stay at the Hermitage. We had become real friends in my first years at Pomona, when he was an elder brother to our Anglican group, and when I converted to the Church of Rome in 1959, he continued to support me. But my running off to a just-founded Big

Sur hermitage of an obscure little Italian order was a bit much for him. As a gentleman and devout Episcopalian, he had couched his questions very courteously, and I tried to be as gentle in reply:

April 27th 1959

Thank you for your kind letter, I very much appreciate your concern that I deal with the crucial questions you raise, and appreciate even more the spirit in which you set them forth.

It isn't necessary, as you observe, to argue you into the legitimacy of the contemplative life. [God bless those Episcopalians who understand these things!] In fact your quiet and unostentatious witness for the life helped quite a bit, I think, in my nurture into the life. And you don't hold, I think, as some, that though the cloistered life has a place, it can only claim the decrepit and soft...and must leave the rest to the active and mixed. As I understand it, you're suggesting, 1) that the Church at this particular time and place has a huge need for a kind of scholarship and teaching, and 2) that's the need God has given me gifts to help meet, so that I should consider hard if this isn't my vocation. As you have prophesied, I must answer that I have considered hard. As you know, I hardly went sour on the technical theology studies, but got more excited as time went on...But of course you know that there is also a great burning need for the continuation of the re-birth of the contemplative life of the Church...Thomas Merton, to consider just the apologetic angle, has drawn more eyes of my generation Catholic-ward than Maritain, Gilson, Dawson, etc. (Please note I have no apologetic motives in my move...I am at the point spiritually that when I've convinced myself I'm witnessing for the Church, I'm later made aware that I'm witnessing for the splendor of Bob Hale)...The Church here and now also has a crying need for contemplatives—and perhaps even a greater need. The central question, of course, is simply, *do I in fact have a vocation?* St. Thomas writes that the postulant is to simply assume he's meant to be where he is. Later he may feel compelled to go over the wall on a moonlight night, or the community might give him the old heave-ho, but still, *qua postulant,* he is to assume the vocation...If God throws me out in a month, or even a year, it's been time well spent...and I will return to the active life spiritually

enriched, and satisfied that I've tried out what I felt bound to try out, and what my Church, because of my conviction, teaches that I ought to give a try if at all possible...
Yours in Christ, Brother Bernard, —Bob.

I remember coming to the Hermitage as a College senior, with the full intention of staying until they threw me out. (Somewhere I had read such a recommendation in St. Thomas Aquinas, and as a zealous convert, I was going to go for it!) Well, I did, and they didn't, so here I am. Which says something to me about the tough wisdom of someone like St. Thomas— how it can determine the course of a life. And it speaks volumes about youthful stubbornness. And about grace.

+

During the first semester of my senior year in college I had determined to try the Camaldolese vocation. I had read in *Time* magazine(!) about the new foundation in Big Sur, and wrote to ask about making a retreat during the Easter break to explore the life. Afraid that it might come to nothing, I did not share any of this with my fellow students or faculty friends. But I did arrive at the Hermitage—a row of wooden buildings and bunk-houses—with the firm intent of staying until they tossed me out. When the monks decided to let me continue, my faculty adviser, Dr. Frederick Sontag, was so appalled (thinking perhaps that I had flipped out under the pressure of final exams) that he jumped into his car and drove up from Southern California to talk me, or the Prior, or *someone,* out of all this nonsense. The Prior was delightful, listened fully to the professor, and encouraged him to speak at length with me. He did, and I was indignant at his suggestion that I was motivated by fear of college finals. He asked, then, why I should not take them here? No problem, I proudly responded. So the professor maneuvered me into finishing my course work (and getting my degree) but he still had to convince the college to permit the taking of senior finals in a Romish hermitage! "If we can't trust *them,* who can we trust?" he pleaded. In the end the exams went sufficiently well to obtain for me the Pomona B.A. and a Wilson scholar-ship and a few other merit badges. What did I need with any of that? I asked myself. But in fact the Camaldolese Order went on to encourage me to continue my studies and get an S.T.B., an M.A. and a Ph.D. That piece of paper from Pomona proved very providential indeed, and Dr. Sontag's continued friendship was invaluable. After my studies in Rome at Sant'Anselmo, he was able to go there and teach some courses as visiting professor there. He became the first Protestant to teach in a Roman Pontifical College. Now he is on our Camaldolese Board of Advisors, our only United Church of Christ minister, (we do have an Episcopal priest too), and he has even encouraged this journal/chronicle project. From dedicated professor and adviser, he has become a close friend.

MARCH 11TH

R uth Martin, one of our oblates who was received into the Catholic Church here at the Hermitage, is a counselor and teacher. She has offered to many groups the workshop, 'Peacemaking and Forgiveness,' and she is here this week to offer it to us.

Her first point today was that forgiveness is extremely difficult. It does not come naturally. Why are we so hesitant to forgive? The monks responded with all kinds of thoughts: fear of rejection, fear of looking stupid, fear of being exploited. I quoted a recent phrase from the politician Bob Dole, battling Pat Buchanan in the primary elections, "I'm not going to stick out my hand to him and just have it chopped off!" Then maybe there are even deeper fears: of acceptance, of reconciliation, of the risk of intimacy, of the loss of the sense of being the victim, of righteous indignation. Ruth conceded that there is a payoff in not forgiving, and we often enjoy clinging to angry isolation, the black-and-white clarity of vengeance. Rancor permits us to remain self-absorbed, pumping up our ego.

One of the monks wondered if withholding forgiveness might be sometimes necessary for survival. If one had been walked over again and again, one more act of forgiveness might be self-destructive. And suppose the father is abusing the child? Does the mother just forgive him?

Ruth stressed that forgiveness can never be acquiescence to evil, never co-dependency in some dysfunctional pattern. One would need rigorously to resist something like child abuse, safeguard the child, but somehow not demonize the offender. Distinguish the deed from the person. "But will the person thus challenged be able to pick up the distinction?" a monk asked. "I never said it would be easy," Ruth replied.

"Isn't forgiveness possible only after the offending party has asked pardon?" asked the same monk. "How can one forgive someone who isn't even requesting forgiveness?" But Ruth and others of us thought that Christian forgiveness, at least, cannot be contingent upon such a request from the other. Christ from the Cross prayed for his crucifiers even while they were in full fury. Our moderator mentioned the need to forgive those who are distant, or even deceased, and who cannot ask pardon. But it is hard, hard work. Cheap pardon, 'just making nice' does not help anyone.

Forgiveness does not give any guarantee of success and happiness in this world. People of peace, a Gandhi, a Martin Luther King, frequently end up crucified or assassinated. But even when the peacemaker is not killed, such forgiveness puts one beyond earthly time into the *kairos* of the Kingdom.

MARCH 12TH

Desert Day. The whole day in my place. The rains encourage staying put. Every now and then, as I'm doing some project, or walking from one place to another in my cell, I have to stop and acknowledge God's presence. Sometimes I'm held in the pause. If it becomes too noticeable, Elizabeth the cat starts meowing, but normally she is very contemplative, a good example.

Sometimes people have to get away from their usual place of living and work. We monks too. But our desert days can be better than a quick break. They carry us back to the center of what our living and work should be, and at the same time draw us as far away as the Totally Other.

> At the still point of the turning world. Neither flesh nor fleshless;
> Neither from nor towards; at the still point, there the dance is,

114

But neither arrest nor movement. And do not call it fixity,
Where past and future are gathered, Neither movement
from or towards,
Neither ascent or decline. Except for the point, the still point,
There would be no dance, and there is only the dance.
                                T.S. ELIOT, *FOUR QUARTETS* [81]

People can go into the rotunda of the church and sit quietly and pray any time a liturgy is not in progress. Besides this informal possibility, every day after Vespers we have an established (but optional) half hour of silence around the altar. Usually there are at least some of the monks and some of the guests, sitting in a circle with the square stone altar at its center, as a striking symbol of our 'still point.' The silence of that half hour can become very deep, and we can feel profoundly united during and after the half hour, in a very mysterious way.

Other monks prefer to pray silently in their cells—and that is what they are for (both cells and monks). For me, solitary quiet in the cell certainly complements the communal sitting in the rotunda. I do miss various things on my Desert Day, and one of them is the silent sitting together after Vespers.

MARCH 13TH

Today we had Ruth's second presentation on nonviolence and forgiveness. Both blackboards were filled with outlines and quotes. Gandhi featured prominently.

Have I that nonviolence of the brave in me? My death alone will show that. If someone killed me and I died with a prayer for the assassin on my lips, and God's remembrance and consciousness of His living presence in the sanctuary of my heart, then alone would I be said to have had the nonviolence of the brave.

                                MOHANDAS GANDHI

Ruth shared some of her personal story, of which some of us already knew part. She had been the victim of a bad car accident a few years ago, suffered brain trauma, and her income was reduced to practically nothing. Her efforts to gain compensation were slow to bear fruit. In December 1991, she visited the Hermitage, and that was the beginning of her conversion to Christianity. On Easter Sunday, 1993, she was baptized in our liturgy, Raniero was her godfather. She is an oblate and worships regularly at Incarnation Monastery, so our bonds are deep.

She has studied Gandhi and nonviolence at the Franciscan School of Theology in Berkeley, and has participated in the demonstrations against nuclear armaments at Livermore (with our Randy, in his full habit, she noted), and has been arrested there. It is difficult to imagine this small, extremely gentle woman being hauled off in handcuffs by the cops, but it has happened more than once. She said today that without her work promoting nonviolence, she could not have gotten through both the car accident and the attendant legal snarls.

Her class today included concrete steps in moving from rancor to forgiveness. First there is the need to acknowledge hurt (not to bury it), then to decide to forgive as an act of will and to activate that decision. In this context, I recalled the theology of love as an act substantially of the will, not just a cluster of warm feelings.

Her presentation, and probably just the topic, stirred up lively discussion. Are there ways in which the structure of our monks' lives, which favors solitude, fosters the unhealthy avoidance of conflict and authentic resolution? Is this merely to put the blame on structures when we ourselves are the issue? The atmosphere of the discussion got very charged. Nothing like the topics of forgiveness and nonviolence to stir up anger! I recall the peace group at the Graduate Theological Union. Our meetings, as we got into tactics and strategies were famous for becoming...intense. A passerby was heard to comment, "Don't worry about all the shouting and finger-pointing—it's just the pacifists!"

MARCH 15TH

Today a group of us—monks, oblates, retreatants, eighteen in all, took the Pax Christi 'Vow of Nonviolence.' It is the ninth consecutive year that some of us have taken it here. I remember Cassian organizing the first discussion, preparation and vow-taking in 1988. The vow is fairly demanding:

> Recognizing the violence in my own heart, yet trusting in the goodness and mercy of God, I vow for one year to practice the nonviolence of Jesus...by striving for peace within myself and seeking to be a peacemaker in my daily life, by accepting suffering rather than inflicting it...by persevering in nonviolence of tongue and heart; by living conscientiously and simply so that I do not deprive others of the means to live; by actively resisting evil and working nonviolently to abolish war and the causes of war from my own heart and from the face of the Earth. God, I trust in your sustaining love and believe that just as You gave me the grace and desire to offer this, so You will also bestow abundant grace to fulfill it.

Some of our monks did not take this vow, saying that it is already there implicitly in our monastic vows, indeed in our baptismal vows. But others of us think that in this horrendously violent century it is helpful to render explicit what is implicit. Others feel it is too Utopian.

By chance I was presiding today at the community Eucharist, and the Gospel was about the Greatest Commandment.[82] I noted that the Gospel was very apt for those of us taking the Nonviolence Vow, since Christian *agape* is not only the fullness of the Law and the Prophets, and greater than 'burnt offering and sacrifice,' and the fulfillment of our monastic Rule, it is also simply what we are trying to live a little more completely through the nonviolence vow. If a Christian really wants to take Christ's New Commandment seriously, does not he or she have to journey in the way of nonviolence?

But I acknowledged that this is one of those 'disputed questions' to which Christians legitimately differ in response.

Indeed, the majority Catholic view, at least since the time of Augustine and his Just War theory, is that in this fallen world we regularly have to choose the lesser of two evils, and this means sometimes, according to this tradition, having recourse to violence. And this is precisely, however paradoxically, out of Christian love. If Hitler's armies are roaring across Poland, is it quite enough to hold up placards and sing 'We Shall Overcome?' I remember a rousing debate on all this between two professors of religion at Pomona back in about 1957. Professor Kaufmann, later to teach at Harvard Graduate School, a Mennonite himself, presented the classical Christian pacifist position. But Professor Halsey, an Episcopalian who drove about campus in a snazzy MG convertible, argued the other side: the horrendous destruction that Nazism had unleashed on the Jews and on all the populations of Europe, required, in the name of Christian love, every efficacious resistance. The various pacifist movements attempting resistance had been doomed to failure, and so represented a tragic, unintended complicity in the evil of Nazism.

Halsey said that he had been too young to participate in the war, but could well imagine a Christian taking a gun and shooting to kill, out of love for the victims of Nazism, and even for the German soldiers themselves, who were better off in the Kingdom of Heaven than waging war for Hitler!

Then there are anti-establishment variations on this argument, I noted. According to this theorizing, as I understand it, institutions as such are often repressive and implicitly violent. They are not going to yield at the first polite invitation. Only by clever, subversive violence of every sort, will the institutions fall and a new, just order be established. As one of our leftist Italian monks used to say: "You can't cook an omelet without breaking a few eggs."

Many pacifists will reply, paraphrasing Chesterton, 'It isn't that nonviolence has been tried and found wanting, it is just that it hasn't been tried.' In those few cases when it was energetically embraced, the most astonishing results ensued: as with Gandhi in India and Martin Luther King, Dorothy Day and Cesar Chavez in the U.S.

Both sides of the argument are talking about the practical efficacy of pacifism, and I am not sure that either will convince the other any time soon. It seems to me that history does not teach that pacifism is guaranteed to lead to success. Jesus ended up nailed to a cross, St. Steven was stoned to death, Gandhi and King were assassinated, and their legacies did not and do not enjoy limitless triumph.

I fall back on a more modest pacifist position: Whatever the practicality of nonviolence (or of Christian *agape,* or of Christian forgiveness), some of us feel compelled to follow this road for the Kingdom of God which is 'not of this Earth.' One thing is certain, there will be no more violence in the Kingdom, no more napalm bombs nor assault weapons nor nukes nor even Saturday Night Specials. I mentioned in my homily that Nancy Reagan confessed to keeping an "eentsy-weentsy little pistol" by her bedside. In the Kingdom there will not be any eentsy-weentsy little pistols. And as our own St. Peter Damian argues, at least *some* Christians have to keep reminding everyone that there is such a thing as the Kingdom of God, that the 'practical methods' of this world cannot become normative for Christians, and *realpolitik* cannot substitute for the radical nature of the Gospel. There is a need for an energetic eschatalogical witness to be offered by at least some. Thank God for the Quakers, the Mennonites and the pacifists of other Christian traditions, and for a Gandhi, a Thich Nat Hahn, who help us glimpse 'a new Heaven and a new Earth.'

MARCH 16TH

Saturday Chapter. As always we began with announcements, principally preparing for the solemnity of St. Patrick's Day tomorrow. We whimsically discussed the possibility of a parade through the cloister, with floats, etcetera. Then St. Joseph's Solemnity is coming up (the feastday of our blind, heroic and prayerful recluse, Fr. Joseph), followed by the feast of St. Benedict (feastday of Bro. Benedict). So the coming week, though in the middle of Lent, will be rather festive!

Then we returned to considering the conferences of Fr. Paul Philibert on chaste celibacy—how the categories of developmental psychology can illumine the challenge, we reviewed those three basic tasks that confront every adult: identity, intimacy and generativity. The identity challenge confronts a young man or woman when it comes time to choose a career. What will he or she prepare to *do?* How is the chosen career to be pursued? Robert Bellah notes that this career approach is a recent development, and it can trivialize the mystery of a person's destiny and gifts. In ancient and medieval cultures, a young man would ponder not career, but *vocation.* He would not be looking at salary and security and retirement benefits, but at where he was destined to serve, for God and for the community. Even nowadays, if one is intending a monastic vocation, one has to revert to the ancient ways. People do not entertain monastic life because of the salary and perks, but because they have been grasped and led by the Lord.

Normally, in secular society a young man or woman seeks to define self-identity in terms of marriage and children and career. The spouse of so-and-so, the parent of such-and-such children who works at such-and-such a job. The monk does not have these profound relationships to expand his self-identity. If anything, he homes in on the 'still point,' the one thing necessary: God. This does not immediately shed a lot of light for him (or for his family or friends) regarding the mystery of who he is. To say, 'I have no family, I am a celibate monk, I contemplate God,' is less satisfying, less clear than, 'Three kids, great wife, and I am a structural engineer.'

Career and familial relationships, even when clearly defined, are not ultimate answers to the mystery of a person's deepest identity. That 'secret name,' given by God, will only be revealed in the Kingdom. It is at least heading in the right direction to explore the mystery by meditating on Christ, the New Man, whom we are called to become in such a variety of ways.

In choosing a career, many young people feel the need to ponder seriously such issues as salary and job security. But there are always some who ask wilder, more idealistic questions: what project or cause is vast enough, sublime enough to embody my deepest yearnings, claim my gifts? What merits the investment of my life? In a monastery we seek to offer the rather extravagant package: the God of Heaven and Earth. It is hard for IBM or General Motors to top that. Most career counselors and aptitude tests do not entertain such a career, but many young people do. Many will end up seeking God in a life of service, perhaps in raising a family or in medicine or teaching. Some will seek God in a more immediate way. Chaste celibacy will intensify the immediacy, it will give an unusual character to a person's identity, their understanding of who they are and who they want to become. Every Christian, every human being is called to this understanding. Oliver Clement writes:

> The human vocation is to fulfill one's humanity by becoming God through grace, that is to say, by living to the full.[83]

MARCH 19TH
SAINT JOSEPH

Today is the feast of the mysterious, very lovable St. Joseph! Isaiah said in his homily that most of us are better at words than action: "When all is said and done, much more is said than done." With Joseph it is the opposite. Indeed, he does not say a word in the whole New Testament. But actions do speak eloquently, especially actions which are not driven by the ego but by directives that come from beyond—even dreams.

Joseph's inspired action unfolds in the midst of much suffering. He almost loses his fiancée whom he thinks has been unfaithful. He loses his home and family as he is forced to flee Nazareth for Egypt, (he is the father of Christian exiles). Then he loses his only son for several days, and he and Mary frantically search the Temple. And after all the silent drama he disappears.

Isaiah suggested that St. Joseph could be the Patron of Last Minute Saves. In all of the above incidents God is working and salvation history is unfolding.

Joseph is also Patron of the Ordinary. The New Testament says nothing about extraordinary asceticism on his part, nor of his working miracles, nor of his delivering splendid discourses. We have no writing from his hand. He is a family man who works for a living, and has the cares of a father and husband. But in the middle of the ordinary are the Son of God and His Mother. St. Joseph is like the field in the Gospel, in which is hidden a great treasure, and his life is the silent stewardship of that field and treasure. He watches over the treasure and rejoices in it. We are called to be that same field today, and rejoice in the same treasure.

+

Today is the first anniversary of the death of Bro. Philip. He had said years before that he wanted to die on this feast because of his devotion to the father of Our Lord, Patron of Good Deaths! For most of his life, Philip was rather tough, a stickler for the rules and regulations. Habitually frowning, he was a holy terror of younger monks and guests. If any woman guest wore a skirt above the ankle, poor woman! He would approach and declare, "Our Lady is grieved by such dress!" A priest retreatant once dared to wear Bermuda shorts to liturgy. Bro. Philip was on his case the minute prayers concluded. "Oh Father, have you no trousers for church?" But as he entered his final infirmity, which lasted years, he mellowed, and became delightfully pleasant. His infirmary cell became the community center of the place, where monks loved to gather and joke with him. A few years earlier, we would not have imagined such a transformation. You may not be able to teach an old dog new tricks, but old Christians, old monks, yes. It was a real miracle, better than a healed goiter. It was a sign of hope for the rest of us: old age can be the best time of all.

So after the Eucharist we processed out to the grave, with processional cross, candles and incense, and Isaiah offered some prayers. Then we opened up to Prayers of the Faithful, with many thanksgivings for the astonishing transformation of Philip. For his smile. For his prayers.

MARCH 21ST
SAINT BENEDICT

Arthur offered a delightful homily about the Patriarch of Western Monasticism. As a good artist, Arthur had walked around our grounds looking for an appropriate visual image of the Saint. The monks worshipping in choir?—I would have picked that!—Too obvious, he argued. A monk receiving a guest at the retreat house? Certainly not bad! Also too obvious, he said. Rather, he proposed the immense old oak down our road, with its vast root system plunging deep into the earth, and its four main branches, each a lateral trunk itself, reaching out with their own branches, and foliage galore. So it is with Benedict and the family that blossoms from him.

+

In the evening some of us gathered for our monthly Poetry Seminar, this time on Walt Whitman's *Song of Myself*. Bro. David Stendl-Rast was also present, with a woman who is part of the respected television news program, The MacNeil-Lehrer News Hour, (she had been at the Hermitage before, with their crew filming a segment on us, as context for Bro. David, who is sought out by the media).

Probably all of us had approached Whitman with a certain diffidence. He can be a bit too boisterous, blustering, posing and posturing. Latest scholarship does argue that he worked intentionally at mythmaking, with himself as his principal creation. Still and all, we were amazed at his courage and creativity, to be able to bust out of the constrictions of nineteenth-century poetry, to shatter every Victorian propriety. He is very focused on himself, but a self astonishingly in communion with all of humanity, all of creation:

> I celebrate myself, and sing myself,
> And what I assume you shall assume,
> For every atom belonging to me as good belongs to you.
> SONG OF MYSELF 1.

We noted that he is emphatically inclusive regarding races, classes, genders, in his celebration of the American, indeed the human community:

And I know that the spirit of God is the brother of my own,
And that all the men ever born are also my brothers,
    and the women my sisters and lovers.

IBID. 5

Growing among black folks as among white
Canuck, Tuckahoe, Congressman, Cuff, I give them the same,
    I receive them the same.

IBID. 6

He plays with a kind of sexual inclusiveness that is startling to normal proprieties:

I am satisfied—I see, dance, laugh, sing,
As the hugging and loving bedfellow sleeps at my side
    through the night,
and withdraws at the peep of the day
    with stealthy tread,
Leaving me baskets with white towels swelling the
    house with their plenty,
Shall I postpone my acceptance and realization and scream
    at my eyes,
That they turn from gazing after and down the road.

IBID. 3

He has an in-your-face celebration of sex, and it is startling to remember that he predates Freud:

Urge and urge and urge,
Always the procreant urge of the world
Out of the dimness opposite equals advance, always substance
    and increase, always sex.

IBID. 3

The sensuality is outward and flamboyant, as if Henry Miller were wedded to Creationist Matthew Fox:

Welcome is every organ and attribute of me, and of any man
    hearty and clean,
Not an inch nor a particle of an inch is vile, and none shall be
    less familiar than the rest

IBID. 3

But the sensuality is especially within Whitman's psyche, in mysterious inner trysts:

> I believe in you my soul, the other I am must not abase itself
> to you,
> And you must not be abased to the other.
> Loaf with me on the grass
>
> ...
>
> I mind how once we lay such a transparent summer morning,
> How you settled your head athwart my hips and gently turned
> over upon me,
> And parted the shirt from my bosom bone, and plunged your
> tongue to my bare-stripped heart,
> And reached till you felt my beard, and reached till you held
> my feet.
>
> IBID. 5

Yes, this is a sensual mysticism, we decided.

Bro. David is Resident Scholar at Esalen Institute, just down the road, a famous center of the human potential movement, of Gestalt and massage and hot baths and such things. We joked with him about how Whitman's remarkable sensuality and proto-New Ageism would lend themselves to any number of Esalen workshops. David quipped back that yes, one of Whitman's lines would be very appropriately inscribed above the Esalen hot tubs:

> Knowing the perfect fitness and equanimity of things, while
> they discuss I am silent, and go bathe and
> admire myself.
>
> IBID. 3

Quite a few of Whitman's lines seem to be twitting the pious teachers of his time, and basic Judeo-Christian faith to boot. But some of the lines are just lyrical, even sublime.

> A child said *What is the grass?* Fetching it to me
> with full hands.
> How could I answer the child? I do not know what it is
> any more than he.
> I guess it must be the flag of my disposition,
> out of hopeful green stuff woven.
> Or I guess it is the handkerchief of the Lord,
> A scented gift and remembrancer designedly dropped,
>
> ...

And now it seems to me the beautiful uncut hair of grave.
Tenderly will I use you curling grass,
It may be you transpire from the breasts of young men,
It may be if I had known them I would have loved them.
It may be you are from old people, or from offspring taken
    soon out of their mother's laps
And here you are the mothers laps.
This grass is very dark to be from the white heads
of old mothers,
Darker than the colorless beards of old men,
Dark to come from under the faint red roofs of mouths.
O I perceive after all so many uttering tongues,
And I perceive they do not come from the roofs of mouths
    for nothing.
I wish I could translate the hints about the dead.

IBID. 6

MARCH 25TH
FEAST OF THE ANNUNCIATION

Arthur, one of our artist monks, likes the quote of
Dostoevsky: 'Beauty will save the world.' That could be
the motto of today's feast. It is a favorite among artists, whether
of Eastern ikons, or of Western medieval, renaissance or contemporary painting. Last September, Raniero and I were in Italy
for the Camaldolese formation workshop, and we spent a free
day in the magnificent Vatican Museums. We were struck by
the number of ikons and paintings of the Annunciation. And
what variety of composition! In some, Mary is seated, doing
her spiritual reading, in tune with the announcement of the Arch-
angel Gabriel. In other versions she is kneeling and praying
with Gabriel standing before her. In some, Gabriel is kneeling
or genuflecting before Mary. One startling Coptic painting de-
picts Mary standing at a Christian altar, as if presiding at the
Eucharist, and Gabriel is there as an acolyte! All of these versions have their own theological truth. Mary might well kneel
before the revelation of God's will, the unfolding of salvation
history through her person. On the other hand Gabriel might

well kneel before the Mother of God. And she does preside in a certain way at the paschal offering of her Son, as she renders possible the enfleshing of God's Word. The Incarnation begins today. Salvation begins today.

We Westerners focus perhaps too much on the Cross as the salvific moment. New Testament scholars such as Durwell have recovered the early theology of the Resurrection itself as the culmination of our salvation: the Father, in raising up Jesus, raises us up to newness of life. But the New Testament and early Fathers also see our salvation as beginning with Incarnation, when God reaches over the abyss of our separation and isolation to assume human nature, not just one human nature, but in some manner all, to redeem us all. Is this then a Marian feast or a feast of Christ? Clearly both, as it is also an ecclesial feast (the Church is the Body of Christ) and a feast about our salvation in the Incarnate Christ.

For Raniero and myself, the most striking depiction of the Annunciation in the Vatican Museum is a bronze sculpture by a contemporary artist. Gabriel is presented as lithe, graceful, leaning towards Mary with his right hand arched, extended towards her, And she, even more lithe and graceful, is leaning toward him, with her arm similarly extended. They seem to be swirling in a sacred dance, a circle around a mysterious center. The work certainly expresses Mary's full, active participation in the event. God does not force the Divine Will upon her, but waits for her consent, her fiat. She is profoundly receptive to the message on high, but in a receptivity that is engaged, enabling the unfolding of the divine plan. And so also for each of us, we are called to receive God's Word into our hearts, in this same active, participating receptivity. In the moment of worship, in the moment of service, in the moment of silent contemplation. We are thus called to join in the dance, with Mary, Gabriel and all the saints down through history, and we dance about the Divine Mystery, that 'still point.'[84]

MARCH 26TH

Financial Chapter this morning. It could be a bit dicey. When monks talk about money, savings, expenses, it is not entirely different, alas, from any other group sincerely engaged in the same dialogue. We have to come up with significant sources of additional income. The number of young men joining our community is a real blessing, but each of them has to be clothed and fed! Too bad the U.S. government does not provide a special welfare check for needy, expanding monastic families! (And moving with that digression, Buchanan has, thank God, faded. So now we will undoubtedly have a choice between the two giants of statecraft, Clinton and Dole).

After the Chapter, I shall be driving down to the Los Angeles seminary, St. John's, to visit our theology student, Cyprian, and meet some of his professors. Have to minister to the diaspora!

MARCH 30TH

In Saturday Chapter we discussed the first draft of the Congregation-wide questionnaire just sent me by the General Council in Italy. It proposes thirty-five multiple-choice questions about our identity, about formation, about interpersonal relations, about the Congregation's ecumenical commitment, and so forth. Though problematical in some ways, it seems to be a courageous and penetrating questionnaire, and should give us much to think about. The results, once tallied by an independent organization, should provide much to ponder for the foreseeable future, and especially for our upcoming Congregation meeting in September, our *Consulta*.

By way of example, here is a question from the Person and Community section of the questionnaire:

> Among the conditions that guarantee the primacy of the contemplative life, the General Chapter has underlined the importance of community relations organized in a climate of serene dialogue and respect. Regarding the relations that you at present experience in community, do you feel yourself:
> • Accepted by all the brethren?
> • Accepted by some, supported or rejected by others?

- I accept the others but don't know if they accept me.
- I feel substantially pushed to the margin.
- I've never asked myself whether others accept me or not.
- Other. Specify.

The above could be part of a psychological test for neuroses! Is it rigorously drafted according to objective sociological criteria? The first and second responses are ambiguous. Is any of us accepted fully by all the brethren all the time? In what sense? Are we talking about full agreement with all we do, hold, are? And, if others do not *accept* us, it does not follow that they are merely 'supporting' us, let alone intentionally 'rejecting' us. The manner in which people fill out these questions will be illuminating as to the quality of community we enjoy (or don't!)

I particularly like the options on the question about Priors (am I particularly sensitive here?)

> Which among the following aspects are the two that most characterize in your community the figure and action of the Prior?
> - He organizes the activities of the community.
> - He has little impact because he lacks an adequate cultural preparation.
> - He is the one who does all the things the others don't do.
> - He animates the spiritual life, but is uninterested in practical questions.
> - He presides with authority and charity regarding the fraternal life.
> - He decides everything for each of us.
> - He loves to live in quiet, lets everything go without intervening.
> - He knows how to listen and dialogue.
> - He does not have the human qualities to preside over a community.
> - Other. Specify.

In some ways the choices seem tendentious, as if intended as thumbnail sketches of some of the Priors, as the drafters of the questionnaire see them. That next to last option, for instance, why does it specify *human* qualities as lacking? Why could there not be a lack of supernatural faith or wisdom or love? And that second option: why does it have to be *cultural* gifts that are lacking? Again, why not the gifts of faith, hope, love? In any event, though this might perplex the Gallup organization, the questions will give us some insights as to where we are now and what we need to work on. This is just a first draft, with the invitation to me to give comments, as visitator. So I'll send them this page, in addition to others already sent.

+

Then we had the draft of another document about formation, which had also just arrived from Italy. It has the same kinds of strong points, the same dynamics, but raises one or two of the same kind of questions. A basic concern of many here (myself included) is that there is a certain emphasis on an academic/ university ethos in the Congregation, a model which grants place of privilege to culture and studies and methods of *lectio* (holy reading), and focuses on our ministerial activities.

At the Hermitage we tend to bring to the fore the 'Trinitarian/contemplative model' which stresses that all is gift, that we are in the heart of a Mystery, and that it is primarily the Father who is always working in our hearts in ineffable ways through the Son in the Spirit. Our objective as monks is not to acquire culture (neither St. Romuald nor St. Benedict had a doctorate) nor to develop skills in a particular field, but very simply to seek God. We seek to be attentively receptive—which is not a passive matter—to the primacy and initiative of God abiding in our hearts and in our midst. We seek to put Christ's First Commandment first.

There are two models that propose different priorities for monastic formation, for the life of the community, and for the life of the monk. The academic/cultural model tends to unfold in an active, *kataphatic* way, through words and actions that assume much importance. The second model is that of the contemplative *apophatic* approach, where stillness and peace and awe and mystery tend to prevail.

Of course the two models are not mutually exclusive. If anything, they are complementary. The contemplative way, without a very solid cultural and theological formation can flip into the weird, the fanatical. (We have had some of that in our heritage!) The academic, uninformed by the contemplative, can

130

become just a head-trip, multiplying words and activities that do not always facilitate deep communion with God. Indeed, in terms of interpersonal relations it can erect hierarchies of achievement that have little to do with monastic *koinonia,* (i.e. fellowship in Christ).

However, the academic and contemplative approaches, functioning together in mutual support, make for a very solid and prayerful monasticism. Both are to be found in the Christian tradition, in the Fathers and in Scripture. But as contemplative monks, it is important for us here to give the primacy to the Trinitarian/contemplative approach.

MARCH 31ST
PALM SUNDAY

Holy Week begins! This is the center of the liturgical year, of Scripture, of our lives! We all gathered, monks and guests, by the side of the retreat house on a beautiful sunny day. Under a huge, scraggly tree, green hills about us, we gathered to remember Jesus, to receive Jesus. We could have been in the Holy Land, outside Jerusalem. And each of us has our Jerusalem inside, *is* Jerusalem. Our daily task is to receive Christ anew as our Messiah, and not to betray him, not to crucify him again.

Bruno, as presider, walked down from the church fully vested, strangely alone. He met our crowd, greeted us, and blessed our olive branches. We had picked up our branches from the pile on a table and we were each holding them like a little banner of faith. He first sprinkled the remaining olive branches with the asperges, then each of us and our branch. Somehow we and our branches were one. Our magnificent young German Shepherd dog, gift of our attorney friends, the Foleys, ran excitedly between our legs. His handler, Michael, tried to quiet him, but the dog heightened the air of expectation. Then we set out singing Hosannas around to the guest house and up to the church.

In his homily, Bruno mentioned the two names of today's feast: Palm Sunday and Passion Sunday. These two names indicate the two disparate strands running through today and all of Holy

Week, and in fact the whole liturgical year. Palm Sunday expresses the celebration and joy as Jesus the Messiah enters into his city. On the other hand, it is also Passion Sunday which we mark by the full reading of the Gospel narrative of Jesus' suffering and death.

Bruno then spoke of two temples colliding: the Temple of Jesus' body, and the temple of Jerusalem. In the last days Jesus had attempted to purify the latter temple, overturning the tables of the money-changers, driving out the traffickers. That was probably the last straw: his presumption at entering the holy place and disrupting its necessary commerce. And so the temple officials determine to kill him. Soon enough his body, the New Temple, would be crucified. But that Temple would rise with a new and astonishing capacity to contain everyone and everything. The other temple of stone and wood would be destroyed. And so it continues, the crashing together of the two temples, in history, in our lives.

APRIL 1ST
MONDAY OF HOLY WEEK

Last evening we watched Pasolini's film, the stark *Gospel According to St. Matthew*. It was shot in black-and-white in the soberingly poor villages and countryside of Southern Italy, and the local people were the actors. The film does express the power of this mysterious personage, Jesus, the intensity of life for those who accept him, and those who reject him. It expresses too the inevitable clashes with the established religious and political powers. Easter comes as a shock and a surprise as the stone is blown away from the tomb and the music of the *Misa Luba* booms! 'Galilean, thou hast conquered!'

Pasolini dedicated the work to the 'Beloved John XXIII.'

If one believes in God, and accepts history as more than illusion or irrelevance, it is almost as if God would *have* to set in motion something like the Incarnation-teaching-suffering-death of Jesus. God would have to come into our midst, into the swirling, polluted waters of history and participate fully in the particularities and ambiguities and constrictions of human events—to be with us all the way. Would not that fidelity carry such an incarnate being to death at the hands of institutional power? God would not be able to leave it at that, would be 'forced' to intervene and blow away the cover of the tomb and raise up that incarnate being, vindicating the fidelity and truth of that life, its redemptive force. If God is love and history is real, Christianity—even given its human limits—seems inevitable.

APRIL 2ND
TUESDAY OF HOLY WEEK

Andrew and Cassian come in this afternoon from Incarnation Monastery. Cyprian arrives tomorrow from St. John's Seminary, Los Angeles. Then Randy and Gregory, their last exams done, arrive on Holy Thursday. It is delightful to have the brethren gather for the great solemnities ahead.

We are exploring the idea of a little monastic shop at the bottom of the road, next to Highway 1. We have to significantly increase our ordinary income, and that might be a way. Pieces of our fruitcake and our datenut cake, with coffee and tea, ceramics by Mark and paintings and prints by him and Arthur, books, tapes, that kind of thing. It all depends on the Coastal Commission, and they are (rightly) rather strict! So the whole thing is very 'iffy.' Our contractor is to see them on Good Friday!

APRIL 4TH
HOLY THURSDAY

Love is life that pours itself forth.
H.U.v. BALTHASAR

Today we enter into the Holy Triduum, the heart of the Christian year, of the Scriptures, of our lives. Today's liturgy includes the moving rite of the Washing of the Feet. The diocesan priest or ordinary is supposed to do it in the parish churches. As Prior, I have done it here for the past eight years. It is more exhausting as I get older, the getting down and getting up for each person, and it is humbling indeed. But it is also exhilarating because each person

whose feet I wash is member of Christ, is image of God, is human being! In the Gospel of St. John there is no account of the institution of the Eucharist, only the Footwashing. Somehow for John they are equivalent, the one mystery of Jesus pouring out his love and service upon us, nourishing us with his own body and blood, cleansing us with his own hand. So we are to offer our lives as food for one another. And wash each other's feet.

Jesus gave us the example, and afterwards he exhorts the Apostles to follow it, in Johannine language—to minister to each other in effective ways. Our mother house, Camaldoli in Italy, was commissioned by the episcopate to explore new forms of liturgy. In the Holy Thursday celebration it has come up with a way to express this second half of the gospel. I find it very convincing: the Prior washes the feet of the monk facing him and the monk to his immediate left, then these two wash the feet of the monks beside them, and so on, down the row, and including those guests who wish to participate. This involves many more people as active participants, and in a moving way the concluding exhortation of the Lord is expressed liturgically.

Some weeks ago our liturgy committee discussed the possibility of this variation, but decided against it on the principle of 'if it ain't broke, don't fix it.' But Camaldoli only argues that the conventional way is incomplete, not broken. Then there was the objection that the Camaldoli way would be a logistical nightmare, though in fact it flows quite smoothly. In jest, Bruno said that it would cost too many bars of soap, with us in austerity mode. Maybe that is the most compelling objection.

Camaldoli does insist that theologically the rite is not religious theater. The Prior does not dress up like Jesus, nor the monks and guests like the Apostles to perform for an audience, but rather they all actively participate. The New Commandment has been written in our hearts, and all of us want to give it outer and visible expression. Liturgy is a way to ritualize that outer expression, render it also as communal worship. And we are all called to love one another, to wash each other's feet in one effective way or another.

Camaldoli does acknowledge that its way of expressing the Gospel in liturgy can seem a bit dispersed and complicated. The conventional way is much more focused, presenting the one primary and astonishing truth that Christ comes to serve us. 'He emptied himself, taking the form of a slave' (PHILIPPIANS 2:7). Footwashing was a service performed by slaves—as crucifixion was a most brutal form of torture and execution reserved for slaves and subversives. Thus Christ frees us, to walk in the freedom of the Children of God, in freedom to serve Him and one another

+

From today until Easter Sunday, the sacred images of the church are covered, the tabernacle is empty. After the evening Eucharist we experience the absence of Jesus. This is an important aspect of authentic Christianity: we do not want so to insist on the presence of God and the presence of Christ and the Spirit, that we fail to acknowledge that our lives are often empty. With Jesus we should plead every now and then, 'My God, my God, why have you forsaken me?' And our earnest prayer must often be that of the end of the Bible: 'Come Lord Jesus' (REVELATION 22:20).

APRIL 5TH
GOOD FRIDAY

There was some drama at our early morning Vigils. The church was particularly stark to commemorate Christ's death and we were practically in darkness as young monks took turns slowly reading six psalms that prefigure in one way or another Jesus' suffering and death. Suddenly, behind us, one of the guests, an older, plump man let out a strong groan and fell over on the bench. We have, thank God, at least two nurses among our guests, and our Ed is a medical technician, and they were immediately at his side. The man seemed to be lifeless. One of the nurses, tried to get a pulse and exclaimed, "My God!" We really thought we had lost him, but then his eyes opened with a start. To questions about his health, he replied that he had a heart condition. Fr. Matthew rushed down to get our visiting M.D., and soon enough they were back. In the meantime, what do we do about the prayer?

We made the call to proceed as calmly as possible, and so we prayed with our thoughts divided. Then the man seemed to be quite better, and the group of caregivers walked him to a side chapel, and we went ahead with the prayer more earnestly. Towards the end I dropped back and spoke with the doctor, who reassured me, and I reassured the others. But it was a very intense liturgy, we were well aware of our mortality!

The Solemn Liturgy of the Passion of Our Lord, at 3:00 P.M., was particularly moving for me. Four of our monks sang the whole narrative of Jesus' arrest, trial and death on the Cross, from the Gospel of St. John. The musical setting was contemporary and powerfully evocative. One of the monks, Cyprian, taking the most extensive part—that of narrator—knows the whole thing by heart, having sung it many times, and having taken part in the original recording. The Proclamation transported me, and I think many present, into another place and time. Is there any story like this? It sums up the human situation and is redemptive.

Isaiah, the presider, who sang the part of Christ, mentioned in some brief comments the experience of a friend in a bar. One of the guys there, thoroughly drunk, was mockingly singing the hymn, *What a Friend We Have In Jesus*. Suddenly it occurred to Isaiah's friend: 'My God, it is true! Jesus *is* a friend of mine and of everyone who will!' The Spirit speaking through a drunk. Today's crucifixion is the witness and pledge of that total friendship, as Jesus himself affirms:

> Greater love has no one than this, to lay down one's life for one's friends.

JOHN 15:13

Then Isaiah carried a rugged wooden cross into the rotunda with all the monks and guests following. The cross was held upright as each of us came forward to venerate it. Matthew, the master of ceremonies, had mentioned beforehand that we would be free to manifest our reverence in any form we wished. The variations are fascinating and moving. A couple of people did the full prostrations, kissing the lower part of the cross. Most knelt and kissed the vertical beam. Some knelt, bowing their head to the floor, then passed by without touching the cross. Some (especially the elderly) stood and kissed the crossbeam. Two embraced the cross. But whatever the form, we were all acknowledging that the Cross is sacred, if not decisive, to our lives.

This day has been particularly powerful for me. In the morning one of our young monks came to talk over various details of his solemn profession which is coming up on June 15th. Among other things we discussed details of the liturgy and lunch afterwards and his giving over all his property to the community. All this is a living-out of the Paschal Mystery.

APRIL 6TH
HOLY SATURDAY

Great emptiness. The tabernacle is empty. The icons and crucifix are covered. Even the rugged wooden cross is no longer there. Just a void. Like the shock at the news of the death of a loved one.

At Vigils we read again that *Ancient Homily for Holy Saturday*. We do not know the author, but the anonymity is its own gift (as with the *Cloud of Unknowing*). Some of the moving phrases:

> Something strange is happening—there is a great silence on earth today, a great silence and stillness. The whole earth keeps silence because the King is asleep. The earth trembled and is still because God has fallen asleep in the flesh and he has raised up all who have slept ever since the world began. God has died in the flesh and hell trembles with fear. He has gone to search for our first parents, as for a lost sheep. Greatly desiring to visit those who live in darkness and in the shadow of death, he has gone to free from sorrow the captives Adam and Eve, he who is both God and the son of Eve.

And so Christ descends to Hell, converses with Adam, calls him and Eve and all forth into eternal life, saying:

> 'Awake , O sleeper, and rise from the dead, and Christ will give you light...Out of love for you and your descendants, I now by my own authority command all who are held in bondage to come forth...I did not create you to be held a prisoner in hell. Rise from the dead, for I am the life of the dead. Rise up, work of my hands, you who were created in my image. Rise, let us leave this place, for you are in me and I am in you, together we form only one person and we cannot be separated.'

The homily then uses a series of poetic paradoxes and contrasts Adam and Christ to link—in a dialectical way—the old salvation economy and the new; and both these ways of being are inside each one of us, so Jesus affirms to Adam (and to us):

> 'For your sake I, your God, become your son, I, the Lord, took the form of a slave, I, whose home is above the heavens, descended to the earth and beneath the earth...For the sake of you, who left a garden, I was betrayed in a garden, crucified in a garden...See the spittle on my face I received in order to restore to you the life I once breathed into you. See the marks of the blows I received in order to refashion you in my image...see my hands, nailed to a tree, for you who once stretched out your hand to a tree. I slept on the cross and a sword pierced my side for you who slept in paradise and brought forth Eve from your side. My sleep will rouse you from your sleep in death. The sword that pierced me has sheathed the sword that was turned against you.'

And then Jesus makes an eloquent invitation to Adam—and to each one of us:

> 'The bridal chamber is adorned, the banquet is ready, the eternal dwelling places are prepared, the treasure houses of all good things lie open. The kingdom of heaven has been prepared for you from all eternity.' [85]

APRIL 7TH
EASTER SUNDAY

We gathered in the early morning dark on the porch of the church, huddled and protecting ourselves against the chill. Then Emmanuel lit the fire which provided us with warmth. Bruno, presiding, noted that we were outside of the church, gathered like primitive men and women around a fire in some pre-Christian rite. Then we would be working with water, awaiting the rising of the sun. He related the whole to a cosmic ceremony of beginnings, we were acknowledging that Christ is somehow there from the first. All things are created in and through Him and are now recreated through His Resurrection. I thought of the Jesuit and scientist, Teilhard de Chardin, and his cosmic vision, back through the eons of evolution, to the origins, and the Alpha before that: the Beginning without beginning that is Source of All. And then, after the unfolding of it all through the millions of years, and the blind alleys and falls, the New Beginning, the breaking through of the definitive life of Christ, our Omega, our Fullness.

+

I presided at the eleven o'clock Mass, and preached that all of life is a setting out, with Peter and the Beloved Disciple, for the tomb. Every day we set out anew. Often we may not have a particularly enlivened faith that the tomb will be empty; Peter did not, nor Mary Magdalen. But we set out anyway, as they did. And when faith and hope do begin to stir within, then we start to run.

All of the liturgical year is a setting out for this empty tomb. Already Advent is straining toward the Lord who comes, and not just the Bambino in the crib, but the Lord who comes into His Kingdom. Christmas seems so special and self-contained and complete, and consumerism seeks to intensify that impression. But a careful study of the infancy narratives reveals that they intentionally prefigure the Paschal Mystery in many ways. With Epiphany, the Wise Men journey from the East, and ultimately they are seeking the King of Heaven and Earth. Lent is all foreshadowing and tension towards Easter. Holy Thursday and its Eucharist are already Paschal. The Lord we receive in the Eucharist is the Risen Lord, we commune in His risen body and blood. Good Friday and Holy Saturday are anything but 'good' and 'holy' except in the light of the Risen Christ. The whole liturgical year before Easter is a preparation for this 'day of days.' All the feasts and solemnities afterwards are the unfolding of the proclamation of the Easter Good News.

If this is true of the liturgical year, it is quite as true of all Scripture. From Genesis on, it is all preparation for, prefiguration of Easter. And so during this morning's Vigils we had nine readings from every part of Scripture, each announcing Easter in its own way. The creation narrative of Genesis looks forward to our new creation in the Risen Christ. The Passover of Exodus is not just a movement of a people to another geographic area to set up another political regime, it is a pilgrimage towards the Risen Christ. The kings David and Solomon anticipate the King of Kings. All the Prophets in one way or another, more or less clearly, are preparing the way for the Risen Messiah. In the first reading of today's celebration, Peter explicitly makes this astonishing claim: 'To him all the prophets testify' (Acts 10:43). Also in the New Testament, all three synoptic Gospels build towards Easter as towards their climax, and every page of St. John's Gospel is bathed in the Easter light. The subsequent writings, Acts, the Letters of St. Paul, etcetera, are simply a proclamation of the Good News of Easter to the four corners of the Earth—to our communities and to our hearts.

So, Easter is the very heart of the liturgical year, and of the Scriptures. And it should be so of our personal and communal lives—the heart pumping the life-blood to our whole being.

+

Easter is, as the medievals said, the Eighth Day after the seven of Creation, the definitive day without dusk. George Herbert expresses it powerfully in his brief poem entitled simply 'Easter:'

> Can there be any day but this,
> Though many sunnes to shine endeavour?
> We count three hundred, but we misse:
> There is but one, and that one ever.

April 8th
Easter Monday

Our four Incarnation Monastery monks left this morning to return to Berkeley and their own life and studies. Cyprian left for St. John's Seminary. It was wonderful to have them here for the solemnities, sad to bid them goodbye.

Easter is salvific—not just an appendage to the saving Cross, not just a proof that the Father has accepted Jesus' saving offering there. Rather, our salvation in Christ begins with the Incarnation, is confirmed on the Cross, but decisively achieved in the victory of the Resurrection, when Christ raises us up from our spiritual death. A paragraph from a powerful Easter homily by Melito of Sardis makes this point. The Risen Christ affirms to all of us:

> Come then, all you nations, receive forgiveness. For I am your forgiveness, I am the Passover that brings salvation...I am your ransom, your life, your resurrection, your light, I am your salvation and your king. I will bring you to the heights of heaven. With my own right hand I will raise you up, and I will show you the eternal Father. [86]

APRIL 10TH
WEDNESDAY OF EASTER WEEK

Our turn today to host the Four Winds Council which consists of the four spiritual centers (analogically, at least) of the Big Sur: Tassajara Zen Center, Windows to the West Native American Center, Esalen Institute, and the Hermitage. Some twenty-four people showed up for an all-day exchange. We clearly share a concern for our common setting, the Big Sur. Government and developers are eager to intrude and 'improve' things.

Raniero and Arthur organized our hosting, which included a little prayer rite at the beginning. The chairs in our Chapter room were in a large circle, and in the center was placed a large lit candle on a wrought iron holder, beside which was a round pan of sand. Long, slender tapers were arranged on the floor which Arthur scooped up and distributed among us. He explained that one by one we were to light the tapers from the central candle and set them into the sand while offering a thought or a prayer, or keeping silent. We proceeded with many prayers of thanksgiving for our gathering, our communion, the beauty of Big Sur, all of nature. My taper was broken, so I thanked God for our brokenness. A couple of the Tassajara Buddhists chose the way of silence. It was a prayerful, meditative beginning to hours of good, amicable exchanges about our four centers, and about threats to the Big Sur.

APRIL 12TH
FRIDAY OF EASTER WEEK

Even in this holy season we are having to work mightily on our budget. Last year we were in the red, though our endowment pulled us through. So we are brainstorming about cutting back in various departments. Just today we decreased the library books/journals/CDs budget by several hundred dollars, after the careful research of the librarian. We are also exploring 'Additional Ordinary Income:' trying for a much wider distribution of our fruitcake and datenut cake, going on the Internet with the items of our book and gift shop, maybe building a little museum with a gift shop at the bottom of the road, maybe importing the various products of our Italian mother house, or producing them here, and so forth. All of these ideas require much fact-finding, and each poses its own problems. It is not easy in the 'real world' of finances. But so many organizations and families are hurting. In a sense we are just joining the human race in a more conscious, intentional way. Monastic 'flight from the world' does not mean escaping into a milk and honey paradise where all is provided without our effort!

+

There were some good Scripture texts at Vigils, especially suited to our current concern with things economic:

> Do not be perturbed, remain calm so that you will be able to pray. Above all, let your love for one another be constant, for love covers a multitude of sins.
>
> I PETER 4:7-8

APRIL 14TH
SECOND SUNDAY OF EASTER

The Gospel of today has the Apostles locked in the upper room, for fear that what had happened to Jesus would happen to them. And suddenly He is in their midst! How do we move from fear to Christian peace and joy? Our Fr. John, in his abundant homily, noted that we do not offer an easy formula

143

to answer that question, but rather a Person, the Risen Christ in our midst. Being locked in a room is not a bad analogy for the state of fear, he said. Fear does lock us in, constricts our movements and horizon. Like those inner-city apartments, with multiple locks, a dead-bolt—fitting images for fear. Fear is like being dead already.

The good news (Gospel) is that the Apostles did not have to work through their fear, arrive at a consensus to unlock the door and go looking for Jesus. Instead, He was suddenly with them. They could not ignore the fact. Christ can come into the deepest locked rooms of our hearts and minds, and from within, give us His peace. How often Christ exhorts his followers: 'Fear not!' And his first paschal gift to all of us is: 'Peace!' Wherever we are, even inside ourselves, Christ is there, within that space, offering us His peace, His life, His person.

April 21st
Saint Anselm

My fifty-ninth birthday! Great waves of affection from the guys and friends, cards, notes, prayers at the liturgies, three cakes today at lunch! I suppose that this has been about my best birthday in many ways. I enjoy and appreciate all the affection. And I am aware, as I head into my sixties, that my main source of life and fulfillment has to be beyond.

I am packing for a week of conferences under the heading 'Benedictine Experience,' offered at New Harmony, Indiana.

May 2nd

Back from New Harmony, a village with a fascinating history, built largely in the early part of the last century by the Harmonists, a Lutheran sect which believed in the imminent Coming of the Lord, and they were therefore given to practice celibacy. They labored some ten years building all kinds of community structures, then apparently decided that the life had become too soft, and moved on. There are interesting parallels with monasticism, certainly the celibacy, the eschatological tension, (though we feel the End of the World comes each day). It is interesting that the Harmonists were so focused on heavy manual work and the hard challenges of life that when things eased a little, they had to move elsewhere. Why not move further within, and do more work there?

The Harmonists were bought out by Robert Owen, and he drew luminaries from all over America to attempt to form an utopian society at New Harmony. The new inhabitants focused on equality and education as the binding forces of the community. It lasted only two years! Somehow, monastic communities, for all their woundedness and fragility, stumble ahead, decade after decade, century after century, held together only by the Spirit of Christ!

Now New Harmony is a retreat and conference center. There I offered six talks to a Benedictine Experience group of about twenty-five clergy and laity (almost entirely Episcopalian). I gave two conferences on the *Rule* itself, then four on the unfolding Benedictine heritage as characterized in some of its most eminent spiritual writers. I spoke specifically about St. Bernard and his wonderful teaching about the love of God; St. Aelred, on spiritual friendship as a privileged place to grow in Christ our friend; Julian of Norwich and her consideration of Jesus as Mother, and love as All; and finally about our own Dom Bede Griffiths, an example of a contemporary Benedictine, who courageously gained an opening to the East. The group seemed to respond quite positively.

+

Flying from Monterey to Los Angeles on the first leg of the trip, we passed over the Hermitage. I was quite moved to see the tiny cells carefully gathered around the chapel and other community buildings. The white roofs gleamed in the sun. It was quite evident, even from that height, that down there that mysteriously ordered community was about something very intentional, very planned—even utopian!

145

MAY 4TH

A lively Saturday Chapter, as we discussed our little rural monastery in New Hampshire, Epiphany. The present Prior, Romuald, is here for a week. He has indicated that he would like to return to Big Sur, and our guestmaster here, John, is prepared to go out and carry on. Romuald will take on John's ministry, so in fact they will just exchange places. Epiphany has been ours for less than four years. In that time we have built up excellent bonds of friendship with the local community and the diocese, and a fine guest ministry has been established. But the life there is not easy, because of the cold, snowy winters and the great distance from us. But John is eager to go.

Cyprian, finishing his studies at St. John's in May, has asked to do further studies next Spring. We are now thinking that maybe he could be at Epiphany and take a couple of classes, commuting to Weston or Boston College. He is open to that, so it means that Epiphany has a little core community from January of next year to May, the very demanding months for freezing and snows.

MAY 7TH

When a man knows he is going to be hanged in two weeks,
it concentrates his mind wondrously!

D octor Johnson, the eighteenth-century man of letters, is said to have observed something along these lines, and I feel wondrously concentrated today. Yesterday a Monterey surgeon looked at a little growth in my right armpit, and took it out. He told me it could be one of four things, and scribbled on the paper covering the examination table, four complicated terms. The good news is that the first three are benign. The bad is that the fourth is malignant. I asked what the probabilities were of my having one or the other. With a certain whimsy he said that in the very specific case they are either zero or a hundred percent for each of the four. Then he added that if he had to bet a dollar, he would bet on it being benign. I was feeling a bit more relieved at that, but then he observed, "I've been wrong before.

A woman had two growths on her forehead, I thought they were both benign, and it turns out that one was, but the other was malignant!" So the anxiety level rose again, as well as my concentration.

We will know the results of the biopsy tomorrow afternoon. This inbetween time is intense. Suppose it is malignant cancer? What might be required in treatment? What if the treatments don't work? Driving home I felt waves of panic, then some deep prayer, even a kind of peace 'that passes understanding.' I have started pondering what would be involved in handing over the various aspects of the Superior's job to our second-in-command, Bruno.

As I was driving up the road from the highway I met him, and filled him in. He seemed none too eager to entertain the transfer of duties (he is not political ambition incarnate), and mentioned reassuringly that he himself had a malignant growth removed once, they just cut a bit deeper than they had planned, and the problem did not recur.

So I don't want to overreact. But the experience is a good fire-drill. Sooner or later something like this will happen, and it will be lethal. As I attend the Psalms and the readings from Scripture in the liturgy, and receive the love and concern of the brethren, I realize that I wouldn't want to be anywhere else for the decisive passing over. But I still hope that good doctor wins his dollar bet tomorrow afternoon!

+

A quote from an elderly Trappist of Vina Abbey:

> Fall more and more in love with Jesus. It will be the end of
> all your problems. Or maybe just the beginning of them!

+

I taught our young 'uns today, and there was a lively discussion about the differences between brotherhood and friendship, how my brothers and sisters are given to me, without my input, but how I can choose my friends, and even terminate friendships. Brothers and sisters share in the one family experience, are conceived from the same gene pool, are bonded in the same flesh and blood; but friends can come from different families and thus different racial and cultural backgrounds. As monks we are obliged to see every other monk as a brother in Christ, since we have in Him the same Father, yet we are not obliged to know every other monk as a friend—though that would be the ideal. The distinction keeps us committed to one another, but without laying an impossible guilt-trip on us, given the difficulties in building real friendship with everyone in a community of twenty-seven monks.

The exchange was so good, and my satisfaction so full, that I realized as I sat in the empty Chapter room after the others had left, that I had quite forgotten about skin cancer and mortality. Things had gotten back to normal during the class. There is an illusion and hubris to that normalcy, and we usually endeavor to keep ourselves in that state, through the bustle and satisfactions and concerns of daily life.

On the other hand, such presupposition of immortality is absolutely correct, in the economy of grace. Christ dies no more, and in him we are immortal diamond.

MAY 8TH

The doctor phoned with the wonderful news that the mole is not malignant. So all my concerns about cancer and lymph nodes and surgery and radiation and chemotherapy are lifted. I have a new lease on life. That expression is apt, because we do have to pay our dues, if we are going to live well, but we are usually quick to agree to the costs, considering the alternative! The relief is very deep. But I want to be careful and explore it a bit. I think that there can be a preconscious conclusion to be drawn from all of this, that God evidently loves me after all. But the test could have gone the other way, and I would have had to battle with the opposite conclusion: that God does not love me, is punishing me—maybe to the point of the death penalty! Either conclusion is bad theology. God does not will cancer, but God can work through its occurrence. God can certainly work through the relief found at its absence, and the continuation of a relatively healthy life.

I do not want to slip back into a life as usual—these last days have been filled with meaning: about the human condition, about my own fragility and mortality. Sooner or later, something like a mole or a stroke will do me in. And God will be there in a very special way, and I want to be there with God. These days have been a rehearsal for that final Morality Play. They were particularly intense because they echoed my brother's last struggle with cancer.

He too had a lump in his armpit, but his proved malignant. There were months and years of treatment. At the end, when he was precisely my age, without hair, emaciated, practically un-recognizable, he went to the Lord. Was that to be my fate? Was it in the genes? All this was passing through my head as I waited for the phone call. I was totally helpless, I could not change the results, no matter how much I wanted. Could prayer change them? That question takes one into a theological forest with all sorts of thickets and hidden bogs. Still, I've been asking for prayers right and left!

Monks have been dropping by to ask the results, our brethren at Incarnation and away studying have been telephoning—and the General too, expressing the concern of the Italian monks. The support and prayers have been a great consolation. I put a note on the board, which everyone saw as they went into Vespers, which turned into a bit of a carnival. A rather abundant woman guest was very loud indeed in joining in the singing, and was quite regularly off-key, making it difficult for the choir to stay on-key. It was fun to trace the waves of fury, then amusement, in one's own heart, and read the same on the faces of the other monks. By the end several were repressing laughter, she was so emphatically off. As Raniero commented, "It was like that saying, 'It wasn't over till the fat lady stopped singing!'" Then at the Prayers of the Faithful I offered thanks for the gift of life, and that Christ might always be our Alpha and Omega (following the Vespers reading from the Book of Revelation). And our delightful Joshua gave thanks "that we will have Fr. Robert around a bit longer." That, after the tension of the off-key opera singer almost broke us all up.

Another philosophical reflection regarding my reprieve: good enough that the dark figure of cancer passed my threshold today and didn't drop in. But what about all those women, men and children who are not so fortunate? The people who are just now packing their things for the hospital? I certainly feel a mysterious bond with them, and the obligation for me to try to live my vocation more authentically. Perhaps I have a little survivor's guilt.

MAY 9TH

In his homily, Louis discussed the relation between salvation and law. In its best and broadest sense, the law does not effect salvation, but observing the law can enable and facilitate our reception of the grace of salvation. An ordered, sober life, does not necessarily make one a saint. A whiskey priest might be closer to God—as Graham Greene knew—than any number of Monsignori whose ecclesial careers are exemplary in every respect. But, all things being equal, it is better to be sober than drunk. Thus, the legitimacy of Christian and monastic asceticism. But the danger of slipping into the ways of 'righteous works' is immense. So, the perennial relevance of St. Paul.

MAY 10TH

Raniero gave a heartfelt homily today. Jesus exhorts us in the Gospel to *abide* in His love. We don't exactly know what this means, but we don't have to know. Just *be* there. In our fears, our anger, brokenness—just be there. Live in that place as Jesus commands and invites us. Add to this the further astonishing revelation that we are friends of Jesus:

I call you no longer slaves but friends (JOHN 15:15).

Raniero then reminded us of the Wisdom text,

Who has found a friend has found a treasure (SIRACH 6:14).

It is fairly easy for us to think of God as our friend—but to *experience* that friendship! And more—to realize that we are Christ's friends. We are his treasure! Christian life may be considered simply the discovery of our dignity, living that friendship.

150

Today is the twenty-first anniversary of Raniero's ordination. I mentioned it during our weekly Chapter on Saturday, but made no public fuss today. Raniero didn't want it. The monastic charism is lay, and he is one of the least clerical people I know. He hangs in there with his priesthood because of the tradition of the contemplative priest who glorifies God and intercedes for all of creation.

+

Our telephone system has been on the blink for a couple of days. Today we were without electricity for a few hours to boot, as the highly-skilled Steve rerouted some of our lines. No lights, computers, fax machine—back to a simpler time! To make his repair, Steve had to be raised up to the service pole on a pipe platform that Bro. Emmanuel rigged on the scoop of his bull-dozer. Precarious, but it saved us hundreds of dollars. To get a cherry-picker or any fancy equipment up here from one of the cities costs an arm and a leg. Steve felt fairly sure he wasn't risking an arm and a leg to make it all possible.

+

I am still mulling over my close brush with cancer. The worst case, of course, would be death in the foreseeable future. As I follow the rhythm of our life here, the community prayer with the wonderful Scriptural texts and the Living Bread of the Eucharist, the silent prayer and the warm support of the brethren, I realize that this is about the best place I could be for the final illness. Drawing close to death is, for the believer, an opening to the God of life. And our life is directly that too.

MAY 11TH

Bruno left yesterday for Osage Monastery where he will give conferences on the spirituality of our beloved Bede Griffiths. Monday is the third anniversary of Bede's death, and friends are gathering at Osage to meditate on his life and message. Bruno wonders if Bede gave enough space in his writings to historical revelation, to the Judeo-Christian Prophets, to St. Paul, to the message especially of Jesus. Bede had been so much

151

struck by the more cosmic and metaphysical insights of Hinduism and he worked out a sketch of a very harmonious mutuality between Hinduism and Christianity *(Marriage of East and West).* But was that synthesis more Eastern than Western, more an absorption into the timeless than an acknowledgment of the specifics of the West? When Bruno posed this question to me, I turned up some passages from Bede's *The Cosmic Revelation* where he stresses the need of a Western, historical revelation to complement the Eastern cosmic vision. I think Bruno is still pondering whether the passages are extensive or emphatic enough. And not just him. But of course no mortal can say everything in precisely the right proportion and balance. What Bede did articulate is pretty profound and urgent to the West, and as he got older he was more and more affirming of the West's invaluable contribution which the East requires.

+

Speaking of the East, but of a part vaster and as mysterious as India, Joseph Wong reported today at Saturday Chapter about his three-month visit to Asia. First he went to Taiwan where he spent four weeks at the Benedictine Priory, researching the Tao and giving conferences on contemplative prayer, the Jesus Prayer, and *lectio.* Then he traveled to Hong Kong, right in the middle of the Chinese New Year, to visit his elderly mother. He also stayed at the Trappist Monastery there, met the famous Fr. Basil Pennington, and gave a workshop (in Chinese) on the Jesus Prayer.

The most exciting and historical part of the trip took place in Shanghai, where Joseph offered five weeks of lectures on Christology and spirituality to the seminarians and sisters of the diocese at the official Open Church Seminary. He was the first monk to teach in the diocese (they loved his cowl, especially with the hood up!) the first to introduce the Jesus Prayer and the first to introduce the monastic tradition of spiritual reading. Last night we saw slide after slide of groups of fascinated Chinese seminarians—there were sixty in the Christology class, and double that number were offered the spiritual conferences. Their daily schedule is similar to ours: Morning Prayer at 6:00, Lauds at 7:00 A.M., daily Eucharist, and in the evening Vespers and a half-hour of

Silent Prayer. But they pray in Chinese, we in English, they under a regime that barely tolerates them, we under a regime that is too officially on the side of God and religion. They are Catholic, but not in full communion with Rome, we, serenely Catholic (at least in some ways). They have all suffered and have been persecuted for their Christian faith, none of us really has. At the end of his class, Fr. Joseph asked the students what themes they liked most in his Christology lessons. Two recurred in the answers: Christ's full humanity and Christ's sufferings as redemptive.

+

MAY 12TH
SIXTH SUNDAY OF EASTER

We had some adventure with two of our three dogs just now. The younger and larger Tristan, a purebred German Shepherd while playing with the touchy Scooter, got his teeth caught in Scooter's choke-collar. Tristan panicked and was choking Scooter as he tried to pull away. It took five monks to calm them, and one of the oblates rushed off to get a chain cutter, with which he eventually managed to cut the dogs apart, Scooter gasping. We gave them lots of post-trauma tender care.

Bede, who is a Menninger psychologist, is about to fly to Louisiana to give a series of conferences to the brethren of St. Joseph's Abbey about interpersonal dynamics. We joked with him that he should be able to get at least three conferences out of the ruckus: two creatures of God playing, getting too rough, becoming locked in a situation harmful to both, and in panic more seriously hurting each other. Only energetic outside intervention was able to resolve the matter. How many human conflicts resemble this! The medievals were fascinated by the lesson of the animal realm—Natural Revelation. But the medievals stressed that we should imitate animal virtues, not their vices.

+

We are approaching the Feast of the Ascension, when Christ is taken out of our sight, and then Pentecost, and the coming of the Spirit. The Sunday readings prepared for all this, and John,

in his homily, detailed the mystery of Christ's departure. It is
not a mystery of absence, he said, but of a deeper presence
within, through the Spirit. He mentioned his intense relationship with his own father, who would be here and not there, concerned and talking about this and not that. When John's father
died, immediately his son had a wider and deeper sense of his
presence. So it was in the relations between the Apostles and
Jesus. John suggested that they could be summed up in the two
prepositions: *with* and *in*. During Jesus' early life, the apostles
journeyed with Him, lived with Him. He is a distinct person
beside them, but with his death and resurrection, and the coming of his Spirit *into* their (and our) hearts, he now abides within
us, and we within him. As the Gospel today affirms:

> On that day you will know that I am in my Father, and you
> in me, and I in you.

JOHN 14:21

One of the things we learn from all this is that little
prepositions can be very important in a Scriptural text. In
English, we tend to focus on nouns, but often verbs and
prepositions are more important.

The main thing in all this is interiority—truly opening the
depths of our lives (our hearts) to Christ, and abiding in Christ
at that level of his life. That is what the contemplative life is all
about. In our relations with one another, an analogous development should occur: from just being 'with' to a mutual
indwelling. That is Christian love.

MAY 13TH

We held our financial Chapter this morning. Our Constitutions require us to examine and vote on our annual
budget. It is a little late this year, as we had to research various
technical points regarding income and expenses. We are in the
red again because of the abundance of new vocations. It is a
good problem to have. People who give us gifts help
enormously, but we still must find additional income. So we
discussed adding five extra guest rooms.

After the Chapter I drove into Monterey to see the doctor who cut off the growth on my arm last week. Today he cut away the six little stitches—they were a real work of art and I'll miss them. (A kid with such stitches would be the star of the neighborhood!) But I will not miss the uncertainty of not knowing whether the growth was benign or malignant.

MAY 14TH

I taught our young monks in formation class today. We investigated various historical models of monastic community. There is the earliest, of the Desert Fathers and Mothers. In the center is the *Abba,* or spiritual teacher, and one or more disciples are in profound relation to him, through obedience. However, the disciples are not so deeply involved with one another. I asked what might be the advantages and disadvantages of such a model, and how do we relate to it? Christopher immediately put the telling question: "How does such a group reproduce itself?" Indeed, dependency on the Abba means that the community dissolves on his death, the disciples go their separate ways. It is a powerfully charismatic model, but, for better or worse, very centralized. The Hindu ashram seems to be similar, with the guru at the center, with bonds to one or more disciples, but they not so profoundly bonded among themselves, and there are no heavy institutional elements.

Then came a model that in some ways is the antithesis of the first. Pachomius, early in the fourth century, founded nine huge monasteries for men and two for women, hundreds of monastics were involved. He provided legislation, oversaw the whole as a kind of abbot-general, and provided for his succession. Such a model is much more institutional, but it is also communal, stressing the bonds of *koinonia* among the monastics. It prefigures the later monastic congregations, with several communities sharing an abbot general. When I put the same question regarding the advantages and disadvantages of this model, David noted that it is certainly a more cenobitic structure, more institutional, the other being more eremitical.

We passed on to the model of the Rule of St. Benedict, which can be conceived as the attempt to take the best from the first two. There is again an abbot at the center of things, with a strong relation to each monk. But there are significant bonds of fellowship among the monks, and the life is structured according to the Rule. Provisions for the abbot's succession are indicated, so the community is also an institution in that it survives the death of the abbot, and can perdure generation after generation, as with the Pachomian model. In all this I was following some good insights of Fr Thomas Keating, in an article he wrote some time ago.[87]

Then I asked how the Camaldolese model is similar to all the above, and how different. Certainly we are Benedictine, so the third model basically obtains. But we are also contemplatives, with a strong eremetical element, and we are concerned not to allow an abba or guru figure to dominate. There may well be spiritual leaders in a community, they may or may not be involved in the institutional leadership, but none can presume the total obedience as the abba or guru. Perhaps in a simpler age or setting, where disciples came from agrarian life, with little education, an experienced and wise leader could claim complete obedience and safely lead such disciples into the way of maturity. But today in the West, disciples come with master's and doctorates in theology and spirituality, they are widely read and have been enriched, perhaps conditioned or wounded by a whole series of urban/sophisticated experiences. And with spiritual guides, however holy and learned, themselves limited, wounded, conditioned, the relationship needs to be more nuanced, according to the Camaldolese. The bond is constituted not so much by total obedience as by discerning obedience, by dialogue and mutual exploration. So among the Camaldolese, according to the wishes of our founders, the abba is simply the prior—'first among equals,' who guides and directs in a paternal, but also a fraternal way, assisted by the senior brethren and Chapter, and in communion with the other superiors of the congregation. At the center of the community is not so much the abba or prior, but the Risen Christ, to whom the prior (and all the other monks) is pointing and tending. Thus, Camaldolese solitude, requires the maturity of the monk to be able to stand alone with the Risen Lord, the superior cannot and should not be there in the cell with the monk. To the extent that we are truly contemplatives, the Risen Lord does have to become more and more the center of the community.

MAY 15TH
ST. PACHOMIUS

I am taking my monthly Desert Day today. No common liturgy, no meals with others, no chatting with the brethren. Just the day in my own cell, with little walks when the others are in church.

Two insights in prayer: first, that the person who is closest to me and whom I know most deeply—more than mom or dad or brother or best friend, is, in fact, Christ. His Gospel message speaks with a penetration and gripping power. He has claimed my whole life, and has been faithful to our bond, giving back to me infinitely more than I to Him. And He is with me throughout the day, however intermittent my awareness or response to Him. This can sound pious-sappy, even a bit kooky: 'He walks with me and talks with me...' kind of thing. But it is true.

And the second insight that came to me today: at my deepest and best, I glorify God. God has made it that way. And with all my limits and fragility, I shall do so for all eternity. Forever and forever.

MAY 16TH
SAINT BRENDAN

Here are some powerful lines from Psalm 72, which we prayed together at Vigils:

> And so when my heart grew embittered
> and when I was cut to the quick
> I was stupid and did not understand—
> No better than a beast in your sight.

157

Yet I was always in your presence,
you were holding me by my right hand.
You will guide me by your counsel
And so you will lead me to glory.

What else have I in heaven but you?
Apart from you I want nothing on earth.
My body and my heart faint for joy,
God is my possession for ever.

There is quite a range of emotion in these lines. But whatever the emotion, the Psalmist knows that God is there and God is all. To relate to God wherever we are and however we are, is true psalmody, true liturgy.

+

I am still pondering after the cancer scare last week, what it would take for me to get through the last convalescence and death. I think that given three things I could do it: lots of grace, faith, and friendship.

+

One of our young monk has donated to the library a whole set of *Time-Life* volumes on World War II—photos and text. A group of us here grew up during the war, and we have been exploring our early memories while skimming through the books, feeling astonishment, horror, but also admiration at the incredible heroism of so many, in so many lands, even unto death. The German and Japanese and Italian troops often showed heroism—misguided, we have to believe. Roosevelt and Churchill and Stalin were no Holy Trinity, we have to acknowledge. But as Reinhold Niebuhr argued in the thick of it all, they were evidently less bad than Hitler, Mussolini and the Japanese leaders. But the millions who had to die or be gravely wounded or to suffer the loss of loved ones over that difference! Would we be able to be here, living contemplative lives, if the Allies had not prevailed? Would there be any Jews around? As one who takes the Pax Christi Vow of Nonviolence yearly, I find such questions particularly tortuous and remain certain that in the Heaven which awaits us, there will be no cannon or bombers or barbed wire. And that conviction strengthens the sense that it is worthwhile being around down here, that all is not only grotesque horror, and at least some people need to witness in a focused way on the peace of the Kingdom.

Christianity does not have a facile solution to such mass tragedy, but the Suffering Servant is right there in the middle of it, and somehow assumes it all in His own crucified flesh, which opens up hope. Hence the photographs of soldiers kneeling in worship even on the battleground, or uttering a prayer over a slain comrade. They witness to a Kingdom beyond the guns. Even in the heat of battle they yearn for more than slaying enemy troops, or raising a flag over enemy territory.

Could our deepest sorrow be our sense of separation from God, the Source of life and peace? The toughest battles have to be waged against despair and the violence that despair unleashes. If in those battles we can persevere with something of the courage of so many soldiers through the centuries, we will be creating the possibility of a more definitive peace than Yalta was able to achieve.

+

Freud's error is the limitation of neurosis to the individual. The neurosis involves all society. [88]

W.H. AUDEN

In a world of fugitives
The person taking the opposite direction
Will appear to run away. [89]

T.S. ELIOT

MAY 18TH

At Saturday Chapter, Bruno reported on his two weeks in Guatemala. Two Californian women who have been looking into the idea of an open religious community, and who were spending the summer in Guatemala to learn Spanish and to get grounded in the realities of Latin America, asked Bruno to help them further discern their journey. He has been interested in

159

Latin American issues for years. He mentioned some fascinating aspects of his visit: first of all, the significant presence of Christianity in the form of the Catholic Church, and increasingly in the Protestant evangelical churches which latter are tied implicitly to local and United States structures of power, as the Catholic Church had been. Then there is the strong Native American culture. In the United States we largely destroyed Native American life, but in Guatemala the Spanish enslaved the people, and they were at least able to survive, and are still very much present in the life of the country, the women with a courage, dignity and flair, said Bruno; but the men often appear beaten down. He spoke of the strong involvement of the U.S. in Guatemala, coming to a head in 1954 when the CIA overthrew a reforming government. Since then the U.S. presence has been subtler, but no less emphatic, economic rather than military. Bruno also mentioned a convent of contemplative Maryknoll Sisters, housed in a building that had once served as a police torture center.

MAY 19TH
ASCENSION

B runo preached brilliantly on the solemnity of the day, and tucked a whole theory of Western Civilization into his homily! And it was still shorter than many!

He began by mentioning some of the ways the Ascension of Christ can perplex us. Is it the distancing of Christ from us and our real history, as He soars aloft into transcendent realms? Is not the whole purpose of the Incarnation to realize Emmanuel—God-with-us? Is the Ascension reneging on this? And what are the dangers of triumphalism here? The Baroque paintings of the feast remind one too much of opera, of tenors on plywood clouds being raised up by wires.

Still and all, Bruno insisted, we should not lose sight of the positive significance of the feast ("Thank heavens!" mumbled some of us more traditional types). Jesus ascends beyond the constrictions of space and time to the Other Side, to Fullness, that which we all profoundly desire. And so Christ is more than ever intimately united with us—now from within, from our center. Christ's glory needs to be more than a word for us, it must be tasted, it must be experienced at the core of our being, we must somehow perceive it beneath the surface of what we see everywhere and in every face. The second reading corresponds:

> May he enlighten your inmost vision that you may know the great hope to which he has called you, the wealth of his glorious heritage to be distributed among the members of the Church, and the immeasurable scope of his power in us who believe...the fullness of him who fills the universe in all its parts.
>
> EPHESIANS 1:18FF

But, Bruno asked, could this feast of power and glory have been understood too simplistically, in too triumphal a manner by the Christian West? Christ ascending in glory to dominate and rule all creation through the power of his disciples—is it this picture we hold, deriving from it the idea that Western Christianity, by some kind of political participation in Christ's rule, is destined to dominate all other religions and cultures? The Spanish conquistadors, for instance, are often seen as soldiers of Christ on a mission to extend His rule over the pagan natives of the New World. As a civilization, the West has, "sat upon the rest of the world...exploited it," Bruno argued. And how much of this ambiguous aggression can take its *raison d'être,* even its momentum, from the ascended Christ?

The remedy is right there in the middle of the Gospel, Bruno said, in the Passion predictions and Jesus' call: 'If anyone would come after me, let him deny himself and take up his cross and follow me.'

The same principle is at the heart of St. Benedict's *Rule:* that to ascend, we must descend through Christian humility. If Christianity abandons the pretense to rule from above, and seeks to serve from below, then today's feast can signify the ascent of all humanity, of all creation with Christ to our common Father. As Christ promised, referring to both his ascent onto the cross and his ascent into glory: 'If I be lifted up, I shall draw all to myself' (JOHN 12:32).

Our Offertory hymn, chosen a week before the homily, was darkly, ironically appropriate. We sang the Taizé version of *Christus vincit, Christus regnat, Christus imperat!* [Christ conquers, Christ rules, Christ reigns].

MAY 20TH
SAINT BERNARDINE OF SIENA

In the liturgical year, this is a strange, in-between time: Christ has ascended, but the Spirit has not yet descended with the solemnity of Pentecost. Arthur, preaching today, noted that we do have the Name of Jesus to carry us over. The Saint of the day made the preaching of the Holy Name his principal mission. In the biblical and early Christian experience, the Holy Name meant the power of God, meant access to God and salvation. So Bernadine reinforced in the West the practice that has so nourished Eastern Christianity, the frequent invocation of the Name of Christ.

The Gospel today was yet again about the Apostles not really hearing Jesus. In his homily Arthur told a delightful and true story of an elderly woman he had accompanied to a talk given by Henri Nouwen about El Salvador. The speaker stressed the tragedy of violence in the wars and financial and family structures of that nation. Afterwards the lady said that she found the speaker interesting, but could not understand why he talked about *violins* so much.

MAY 26TH
PENTECOST

Today is a great solemnity, and the bright red stole and the even brighter red shirts of two of our guests helped us get charismatic. And Daniel's fiery homily did too: the Spirit as fire, which causes us to thirst. Mundane cravings distract us from our real yearning, and all consumer society in alliance with our cravings. But the Spirit can penetrate to our inmost heart and revitalize that fundamental thirst for our All.

The Holy Spirit has been termed the 'forgotten member' of the Holy Trinity. And in the West we have been so word-oriented, and thus so cerebral, so institutional and structural that the Spirit has not always flourished. The Charismatic Movement at its best recalls this complementary dimension of freedom, inspiration, the prophetic, the heartfelt. I remember a student at Fordham who rejoiced in her discovery of charismatic worship. Our normal liturgies, she lamented, "are not celebrations but cerebrations." So many rubrics, so much rote, and so many men up there on the sanctuary, carrying-on cerebrally, and so many women down in the pews, aching in their hearts. The Spirit is shaking up things in our own time. As Pope Paul VI affirmed, and as the present Pope repeated(!) Vatican II has been for us a second Pentecost.

These are some lines of invocation to the Holy Spirit from St. Symeon the New Theologian:

> Come, true light.
> Come, life eternal.
> Come, hidden mystery.
> Come, treasure without name.
> Come, reality beyond all words.
> Come, rejoicing without end.

JUNE 2ND
TRINITY SUNDAY

Karl Rahner commented that if the ecclesial authorities were suddenly to remove the Holy Trinity from the dogmas and discourses of the Church, many Catholics would perhaps, alas, feel no loss whatever. Jesus, yes, we need Him, and certainly Mary, and St. Joseph and St. Anthony, and all the rest of the Saints, and the Pope and the cardinals, bishops and priests. They are all indispensable to Roman Catholicism. But the Holy Trinity? Father, Son and Spirit, Three Persons, One God. How on Earth does that have anything to do with us?

I like Rahner's suggestion, and others', that humans have a fundamental Trinitarian 'shape'—since we are created in the image of God, and God is Trinity. Theologians and mystics have, down through the centuries, wrestled with how to spell out that Trinitarian shape of humans. Certainly there is a Word/mind side to us that yearns for wisdom, knowledge and clarity as a means into the Godhead. There is also a Spirit/heart side to us which aspires to love and freedom as ways into the same Godhead. If by 'Father' we mean that ultimate, ineffable Source of Word and Spirit, of our mind and heart, and also their ultimate Fulfillment, then we are daily, and perhaps at each moment, existentially caught up in a Trinitarian dynamic.

And, of course, all of Scripture, all of Salvation History, and every liturgical celebration has this fundamentally Trinitarian dynamic: all coming forth from the Creator and Source of all, through the Word, in the Spirit (mysteriously hovering over the primordial waters). Now all returning through Christ the Word in the Spirit to our loving Father. That is the basic structure of Revelation, and of Eucharist—and of the journey of each one of us.

JUNE 7TH
SAINT ROBERT OF NEWMINSTER

My feastday today, with lots of fun and celebration. Some of the more mischievous monks insist that no one ever heard of St. Robert of Newminster. Ignorance is such a sad thing.

I am reading a recent biography of the poet W.H. Auden, which is quite startling and sad in many respects. But when I picked up the latest Episcopal diocesan newspaper, I saw that the Bishop in his column was recommending that very book to the faithful! Things are changing with the Episcopalians. I cannot imagine my Aunt Gertie, Episcopalian, daily communicant, sitting down to a good read with *Auden.* He was Anglican, but not a very...proper one! And the latest *National Catholic Register,* that arch-Catholic paper, has an article appreciative of the book and of the poet.

Indeed there are profoundly Christian, and even heroically Christian pages to Auden's life. He struggled and suffered as much as any of us, and wrote eloquently of the need to just hang in there:

165

> The task of revealing the hidden field of experience, of understanding and curing by love, is a very slow, but ultimately the only satisfactory one. 'The chief sin,' wrote Kafka in one of his aphorisms, 'is impatience. Through impatience man lost Eden, and it is impatience that prevents him from regaining it.' People take to violence because they haven't the strength and nerve to be absorbent.[90]

Somehow even our modern self-sufficient world is built on the sacrifice of the innocent victim,

> on whose immolation (call him Abel, Remus, whom you will,
> it is one Sin Offering) arcadias, utopias, our dear old bag of a
> democracy are alike founded:
> For without a cement of blood (it must be human, it must be
> innocent) no secular wall will safely stand.
>
> W.H. AUDEN, *VESPERS*

JUNE 8TH

Today we were offered a lovely meditation by Isaiah on the Gospel of the poor widow putting into the Temple treasury her offering, a tiny gift, but representing her entire savings. The widow is Christ, who having become poor for us, pours into our hearts—His treasury—all that He has to offer.

JUNE 9TH
CORPUS CHRISTI

The whole Catholic world today celebrates Christ present in the Eucharist. In many Latin nations the festivities are particularly colorful. We had a solemn homily from Joseph Wong which explored the more contemplative depths of Eucharist. He noted that there are a great many dimensions that could be considered: the Eucharist as sacrifice, the Eucharist as memorial, as nourishment, as bond of communion, and so on. But Joseph focused on the theme dear to the Christian East: the Eucharist as source of our transformation, of divinization.

166

I had kidded Joseph in the sacristy before the Eucharist, saying I certainly hoped he would defend and promote transubstantiation in his homily. He was able to respond, both within and after the homily that yes, he was promoting transubstantiation, and not only of the bread, but of *us* too. He also quoted Teilhard de Chardin, from his *Mass on the World,* regarding a mysterious extension of the efficacy of the Eucharist to all of creation, and the consequent assumption of everything into this transformation into universal Eucharist. Then Joseph touched on the Jesus Prayer as the extension throughout our day of the same eucharistic transformation. To invoke the words over the bread and wine, and to invoke the Name of Jesus within one's heart—these are ultimately one extended prayer.

+

I am reading the seventeenth-century mystic, Angelus Silesius. I love his very brief poems, often enough couplets. They are short enough and intense enough to break through into insight. He loves creation's varied and vast beauty, appreciated not just as lovely in the romantic sense, but as rooted in God's beauty and in awe. [91]

The Rose
The rose which here on earth is now perceived by me
Has blossomed thus in God from all eternity. [1:108]

Creation continues each day, also through the suffering and death of each day:

The Hidden Source
Who would have thought of this! The darkness brings forth light,
The something comes from naught, death does engender life.
[4:163]

The penetrating vision of faith encounters the divine in the smallest speck of creation:

God's Splendor is Everywhere
No speck so tiny is, no spark can be so dim,
The wise don't see God's splendor deep within. [4:160]

For Silesius, creation's great variety is connected organically, each part interpenetrating the other. The poet, tapping Benedictine sources, was an early prophet of 'deep ecology,' and with a mystical depth:

167

All in All
How saw Benedict all in a sun-ray revealed?
See, all is hidden in all, and therein is concealed. [4:159]

Though he can be quite metaphysical in his speculations, there is also a tender love of the crucified Jesus that echoes Thomas À Kempis' *Imitation of Christ,* one of Silesius' sources. That love again carries him to the depths of divinity.

On the Wounds of Christ
I look upon Christ's wounds as wide celestial gates
And know that I can enter through these five safest ways.
How may I come straightway to stand close to my God?
I shall through feet and hands enter the heart of love. [4:46]

In the great medieval and patristic tradition, Silesius also articulates a wonderful, spousal mysticism through the language of its main source, the Canticle:

The Song of Songs
The king leads his bride into the cellar for wine
That she may choose what most delights her taste.
If you would be God's bride, He will deal with you thus;
Nothing He has Himself that He'll not to you entrust. [4:88]

But for all his compact eloquence, the poet is pointing beyond words, is unsaying into the ineffable:

The Silent Prayer
God far exceeds all words that we can here express
In silence he is heard, in silence worshipped best. [1:240]

And he also echoes the highest mystical tradition in suggesting that prayer ultimately concerns divinization.

The Noblest Prayer
The noblest prayer will one so much transform
That he becomes himself that which he does adore. [4:140]

JUNE 12TH
SAINT PARISIO

This amazing Camaldolese saint, born in the second half of the twelfth-century, entered the monastery at the tender age of fifteen, then, after ordination, spent some eighty years ministering to Camaldolese nuns in the double monastery (that is, of monks and nuns) in Treviso. He challenges many of our constricted notions: that monks should not be priests, that they certainly should not minister to nuns, that they should not live in urban monasteries with nuns, etcetera. Sometimes our past is much more radical than our present, our tradition more radical than our imaginations.

+

More gems from Silesius:

I Must Be Sun
Myself, I must be sun, whose rays must paint the sea,
The vast and unhued ocean of all divinity. [1:115]

Why God Has Joy and Rest
Because God is Triune, He does have joy and rest:
Rest is in the Oneness, joy among the Three. [5:283]

Beauty Derives From Love
Beauty derives from love, even God's face
From love originates, or it would radiance lack. [5:292]

The Greater The Love, the Greater the Blessedness
The measure of all bliss one does by love assess
The more one has of love, the more one will possess. [5:295]

JUNE 13TH
SAINT ANTHONY OF PADUA

We are in the last stages of preparations for the three solemn professions on Saturday. Randy, Raniero and Benedict have had countless planning meetings among themselves, with me, with Matthew–the master of ceremonies–with work

169

crews, etcetera. The refreshments have been bought. Mark, the cook, is starting to think about forty-five pounds of pasta. We are praying daily for appropriate weather, neither June-gloom cold and fog, nor hot and humid. There will be about one hundred and twenty-five guests along with the forty of us, crowded into the church rotunda. Our M.D., Scott, and nurse Ed have been trying to anticipate every kind of medical nightmare, from snake bite to poison oak to heart attack. But it should be a glorious day. Christopher is in charge of the team that will make all the practical things happen when they should. Some of the monks are suggesting that in the spirit of the Olympics which begin next week, we should have a second team to inject some good American competition into the whole thing!

Raniero's and Benedict's families start arriving today from Maryland and Pennsylvania. Then Randy's folks fly in tomorrow from New Jersey, with brothers converging from New York and California. It is the monastic equivalent of a triple wedding, the spouse being God.

We are now working on the details of the details. Randy and Raniero are incredible detail men, while Benedict thinks more of the big picture. There will be a sign at the bottom of the road indicating more clearly the turnoff for the guests. I joked that such signs sometimes have balloons connected to them. Raniero replied that he had indeed purchased three balloons: white, the Camaldolese color, grey because the programs are grey, and apparently blue-green is the 'in' color this year. I am relieved that we monks are 'in!'

JUNE 15TH
IMMACULATE HEART

Today is a very special one for the life of our American Camaldolese. Not just because this is the feastday of the Hermitage, which is dedicated to the Immaculate Heart, but also because three of our men offered their solemn vows at Eucharist.

We began with a half hour of silent prayer in the rotunda for those wishing to participate, and that helped many of us quiet down and rededicate ourselves to the Lord, in solidarity with Randy, Raniero and Benedict.

The liturgy was pure joy—with some tears—for the one hundred and seventy-five people present: monks, families, friends. The three young monks had been working on the details for almost a year, and we regularly kidded them about it. But today it all came together, and things moved so smoothly that everyone was able to enjoy the occasion to the maximum.

The Gospel text has the young Jesus in the temple asking his parents: 'Did you not know I must be in my Father's house?' (LUKE 2:49). Why should they have known? What was this strange compulsion requiring Jesus to be there. And what, in the final analysis, is this house of the Father? Certainly the Jerusalem temple, but later Jesus will refer to his own body—that is, His full humanity—as the Temple: 'Destroy this Temple and I shall raise it up again' (JOHN 2:19). And in fact the Word needs to dwell in the fullness of His humanity, as in the Father's Temple, the Father's house, so as to dwell with us, and we with Him, in the one house of the Father. That is the whole purpose of Incarnation. So that our bodies, our humanity also becomes God's house, God's Temple. 'Your body is a temple of the Holy Spirit within you' (1 CORINTHIANS 6:19).

All this is relevant today because these three men are very much in touch with their humanity. Solemn vows is not for them, or for us, an alienating movement away from their humanity, a zipping off into some angelic sphere, but rather a moving into the very heart of their humanity, and ours, there to find God's new covenant of love written on their hearts, and to respond lovingly with all their hearts.

The three prostrated before the altar during the Litany of the Saints, with their arms extended, so that their prone bodies were three living crosses. Their hoods were over their heads, so that all we could see were monastic cowls and bare feet. How they breathed was a mystery to everyone. I saw Randy's father looking down at him with some concern. During the Sign of Peace, the congregation exploded in a celebration of solidarity and congratulation.

In the afternoon, Cyprian offered a concert of his own music in the rotunda, with the guests sitting around the walls. His singing was electric, and at the end there was a long standing ovation, with shouts of *encore!* But he just disappeared.

The food was simple but tasty, cooked with love. Mark had worked from the evening before to prepare the mounds of pasta, salad, cheeses, beverages (no alcohol—we didn't want our guests even a little blotto trying to negotiate Highway 1). Many of the guests ate outside under colorful awnings which we had rented for the day. Others chose the refectory. The three had organized to the last detail the lines to the food tables, where the monks would be greeted, restrooms for men and women (we don't usually worry about the latter!) litter cans, etcetera. Within this framework, people wandered about greeting one another, and of course Randy and Raniero and Benedict were engulfed. Flash-bulbs were popping, Hermitage dogs and cats were paraded. A little foretaste of the Kingdom. It don't get much better than this!

JUNE 22ND

I got up this morning aware of some inner anguish and darkness. I tried to acknowledge it, trace it, but could come up with no specific causes. So I thought to just use that experience as a space to be with God, and it turned out to be a very favorable context. By mid-morning the darkness had passed and I was happily involved in doing this and that—and less aware of God!

JUNE 24TH
SAINT JOHN THE BAPTIST

Cyprian and I went into town this morning for an appointment with our Bishop Sylvester Ryan. We had faxed him Cyprian's transcripts with his latest grades, and the agenda was to discuss whether the Bishop would require more classes as precondition to ordination. Well, nothing of the sort, it turns out. He invited us in, very punctually, at ten o'clock, he warmly supported all Cyprian had done, and said there would be no further requirements. And we were out in ten minutes! We had both noticed on his desk a plaque:

IRISH • POPULIST • RADICAL

+

Then we visited my skin doctor for a last checkup. Everything was okay. He had the file open and I saw the before-and-after pictures of my armpit, the first with that menacing little growth. I am quite delighted to be in the after phase.

We had taken the doctor a bag of our goodies: a datenut cake, a lovely hand-wrought ceramic bowl by Mark, and one of our gemstones. He thanked us profusely, said he was always available to help us out. We survive through the generosity of such doctors, dentists, shopkeepers. They are monks too.

+

In the afternoon Joseph Wong came in with some correspondence questions, and I noted that we had to start thinking about reserving guest space for his transfer of vows, ten months from now. We came up with the weekend of April 26th next year. He will need every guest space we have, with his large family and all his friends.

These moments of planning such happy events are certainly joyful, to say nothing of the events themselves.

JUNE 27TH
SAINT CYRIL

I am back from Incarnation, where I spent some extended time with our Peter-Damian, who has come there for some days from Epiphany Monastery. We have a new long-term guest at Incarnation, Dennis, a Benedictine from St. John's Abbey. He is completing a doctoral dissertation on Hegel. Dennis seems to represent St. John's at its best: erudite, insightful, ironic, prayerful. When he reads the lesson in Lauds or Vespers, you know you are listening to the Word of God.

Andrew, our monk from Italy and the Prior at Incarnation, is going through all sorts of torture as oral surgeons spend hours and hours on his teeth. But he is bearing it with an almost Anglo stoicism!

As I mentioned before, the setting of the Monastery is amazing. It is just a few minutes from the campus, but it is surrounded by trees and adjacent to a charming little park. The overgrown vacant lot next door is anything but vacant. Last time I was there we admired four deer enjoying the overgrowth. This time it was three beautiful foxes.

JUNE 28TH
SAINT IRENAEUS

R aniero, in his warm homily remembered the famous quote from Irenaeus: 'The glory of God is the human fully alive.' And also our life is our vision of God. Like St. Cyril, yesterday, St. Irenaeus was committed to exploring the mystery of the conjunction of the divine and human in Christ, a mystery that is continuing today in us, as Raniero, citing Bruno, reminded us.

+

Tonight I offer the first of four conferences this weekend on Thomas Merton. The retreat house is packed—seventeen people, with twelve on the waiting list! I have to admit that it is Merton who is pulling them in. My conferences last year on Christian love were not such a draw. Merton is bigger than Christian love!

In my first conference I shall note how he insists that all his interests, all his writings, want to come back to the one 'root truth' that God calls us to deepest communion, and that this should be the 'experiential ground' of our lives, the center that holds it all together, the wellspring that can then pour out in so many enriching directions. Without this center and ground, the ego cannot hold life together. Without God, what Yeats writes of this age is true of each of us:

> Things fall apart, the center cannot hold,
> Mere anarchy is loosed upon the world. [92]

If we can return to the center, things do hold together, and a kind of divine anarchy is loosed upon our personal world. Merton writes eloquently of this center:

> At the center of our being is a point of nothingness which is untouched by sin and illusion, a point of pure truth, a point or spark which belongs entirely to God, which is never at our disposal, from which God disposes of our lives, which is inaccessible to the fantasies of our own mind or the brutalities of our own will. This little point of nothingness and of *absolute poverty* is the pure glory of God in us. It is, so to speak, His name written in us, as our poverty, as our indigence, as our dependence...it is like a pure diamond, blazing with the invisible light of heaven.[93]

JUNE 29TH

The conferences on Merton are going well. I am exploring with the retreatants Merton's distinction between the deep, true self, on the one hand, and the false self, or ego, on the other. We are considering how the true self is also the poor, naked, wounded self, terrified of death and horrified by the awareness of personal sin, and how we therefore inevitably try to flee this painful *I*, by running outward to the self-assured, competent, controlling *me*, at the center of my world. We are seeing how our society, through its institutions and ideologies of competition, through consumerism and Madison Avenue, encourages that flight, and the consequent life of alienation and illusion. Then things are further fortified through the collective ego, where I merge my lies with those of others, to become the great *us*—whether that be a gang, a firm, an army, whatever—even a family or monastery! There is the need for conversion, and the painful journey back into the heart, back to where we are weakest, and where, consequently, Christ is, to make us divine.

We looked at how Merton's centeredness enables him to then reach out in so many directions, and so fruitfully, now with a contemplative depth to whatever he undertakes, whether writing prose, or poetry, or taking photographs, and so on. And Merton is also able to open up prophetically to the world's needs:

> To be a solitary but not an individualist: concerned not with merely perfecting one's own life (this, as Marx saw it, is an indecent luxury and full of illusion). One's solitude belongs to the world and to God...Solitude has its own special work: a deepening awareness that the world needs. A struggle against alienation. True solitude is deeply aware of the world's needs. It does not hold the world at arm's length.[94]

JULY 2ND

R andy offered us a conference entitled Moral Theology Today. It was a synthesis of his year's course at Berkeley. He talked of the sacredness of the conscience, quoted St. Thomas Aquinas that one would need to follow one's conscience even if it meant excommunication and death! But, on the other hand, there is the need for an informed conscience, and acknowledgment of the place of the magisterium. Then Randy covered the gradations of authority and the weights of various magisterial documents, (I remember our Fr. Vagaggini saying at Sant' Anselmo that a full semester course could be taught just on that!)

We heard about the emphasis, certainly after the Council of Trent, on individual sins, and the rediscovery, especially after Vatican II and liberation theology, of social sin, and the social structures of sin. Randy also explored nonviolence and the Just War theory; the difficulties of interpreting Scripture and Tradition in the formulation of social justice positions—how long it took Christian communities to discern that slavery is absolutely unacceptable; how long women must continue to be subordinated to men, etcetera.

The presentation was lively and articulate and carefully prepared. Randy has a couple of years more studying for his master's degree. But he could thereafter go on to a doctorate and to teaching. For our part, it is important for a community of contemplative monks to wrestle with these issues, to become aware of how we might become entangled, if only in unconscious complicity, in structures of injustice.

The Gospel today is about the great storm that suddenly arises, the terror of the Apostles in the boat, Jesus who quiets the waves, the great calm resulting, and their consequent awe (MATTHEW 8:23-27). In preaching (one of my shortest homilies!) I noted how carefully crafted the passage is, with the terror of the Apostles because of the *great* storm, and their awe because of the *great* calm. Matthew uses the same adjective for *great* at the beginning and end, to frame the drama, note the transformation wrought, not by the Apostles or their resources, but by Christ. But then Christ remonstrates with them, insists that they too could still such storms were their faith sufficient. How many storms buffet our existence: in the world, in our Church, in our communities, in our hearts? In those moments we fall into terror, but Christ is in the same boat with us. And He does have the power to still such storms, and we also, if we trust in Him. What we are hoping for as contemplatives, what our asceticism should be geared towards, is that 'great calm,' that stillness which is still the milieu of awe. Thus the whole Eastern Hesychast tradition, the goal of achieving tranquility of body, mind and spirit. But to persevere in prayer, also during the storms!

JULY 4TH
INDEPENDENCE DAY

We Americans of the community are celebrating, somewhat sheepishly, our country's birthday. Joshua wore his army uniform to lunch, medals and all, to the amused delight of everyone. But the Eucharist readings were all about peace. And the amazing second reading at Vigils, from a sermon attributed to St. Peter Chrysologus, carried that peace theme to the depths of the heart, making it the sum and substance of the Christian, certainly of the contemplative life. Some passages:

> *Blessed are the peacemakers,* the evangelist said, dearest brethren, *for they shall be called the children of God* (MAT-THEW 5:9). Truly Christian virtue grows in a person who enjoys the unchangeable possession of Christian peace, nor does one come to the title of Child of God except through

177

that of peacemaker. Peace, dearest brethren, rescues us from servitude, provides us with freedom, changes our identity before God, changes our condition from servant to child, from slave to one who is free. Peace among brothers and sisters is the will of God, the joy of Christ, the contemplation of holiness, the rule of justice...a praiseworthy discipline in every regard. Peace lends strength to our prayers, enables our petitions to reach God easily...it is the plenitude which fulfills our desires. Peace is the mother of love...Peace must be preserved according to the Lord's precepts, as Christ said, *I leave you peace, my peace I give you*, that is, as I left you in peace, so in peace I should find you. [95]

+

I am engaged in a rousing debate, via fax, with an oblate and good friend, regarding social justice and the best way to help the poor. She is a dedicated Catholic and a skilled and articulate attorney (who gives us much help *pro bono)* and describes herself as a classic conservative who is sceptical of government far away in Washington and its Big Daddy schemes such as Affirmative Action; she much prefers local initiatives.

I am arguing that the Vatican II principle of subsidiarity seeks to favor local initiative whenever possible. But when the social problems and challenges quite transcend the capacity of local initiatives, then we must have recourse to national, even international efforts—not to localize evil, or good, at any of the levels, but to try to determine how best to confront any specific problem. And we must not forget the principle, affirmed even by the *Catholic Catechism* of a 'preferential love' for the poor. [96] Then there is the fundamental Catholic idea that the abuse of a thing does not eliminate its legitimate use. That is absolutely essential for the ongoing life of the Church!

In this debate we have been wrestling over segregation in the South and the intervention of the Supreme Court from Washington, the Kennedys sending in troops against Wallace, and so on. Then we debated the current ballyhoo between Dole and Clinton over smoking, Dole questioning the Surgeon General, while at the same time receiving big bucks from the tobacco industries. Tobacco is bad news for health in so many ways—

and there are so many billions of dollars invested in that business. Can a local mayor or town council handle that evil cartel? (My mom and dad smoked, with the inevitable consequences, so I am not indifferent to this issue!)

JULY 10TH

For a few days I am staying at our Incarnation Monastery, our urban house with its serene views of San Francisco Bay, deer and foxes in the adjacent lot, but urban, ten minutes walk from the university. Thus it is ideal for our house of studies. I am here briefly before flying off to Epiphany in New Hampshire, there to meet the Visitator from Italy, D. Alessandro, for the official beginning of our houses' visitation. This is a kind of three-yearly verification that the Order builds into our community life. People (including me) are a bit twitchy, but the challenge to growth is a good one. And then I am Visitator for the houses in Italy, so in less than two months I shall be over there, returning the favor!

JULY 11TH

Our Australian novice, David, who has his doctorate in liberation hermeneutics, drove me to the airport for my flight to Epiphany. On the way we talked about deconstructionism. At its worst it can be nihilistic, leading into the destructive void. At its best it can be a kind of negative philosophy, acknowledging the inner limits and even contradictions of any human construct, and thus, at least implicitly, opening out to a real Transcendence.

JULY 14TH

Now I am safely unpacked at Epiphany, our eighteenth-century farmhouse-made-monastery. There have been long meetings with Alessandro and our monks here, Romuald, Peter-Damian and Zacchaeus. We Camaldolese have been here a little over three years, but the local support is already very substantial. We all hope the house can make it.

JULY 15TH

My sister-in-law phoned me at Epiphany: my older cousin, Derald, died of cancer last night. He was the family atheist, did not want any kind of memorial service. He donated his body to the University of Colorado for cancer research. The family does not quite know what to do to commemorate him, to grieve as family. We Christians make it easier for the survivors! But I do appreciate his wanting to make it easier for cancer victims by offering his body. He really believed in life this side of the pass. That might well be enough to get him across into the fullness of life.

JULY 19TH

Back in Berkeley. Hours of discussions with Alessandro and the monks of Incarnation. Our urban house of studies is so different from Epiphany in the New Hampshire woods, and radically different from our Big Sur Hermitage. But there is the same basic Camaldolese life lived in each place: the unfolding of the daily liturgy, community life, silent prayer, hospitality, etcetera. Alessandro is as committed to our city monastery as to our two other houses, and our three correspond to the three main Camaldolese houses in Italy: the Sacred Hermitage and Monastery in Tuscany, and San Gregorio Monastery in Rome. Diversity in Unity seem to be characteristic of Camaldolese.

JULY 28TH

Now I have returned to the Hermitage, and am recovering from a week of visitation here. Fr. Alessandro finished today, and I drove him up to Incarnation. Sometimes we get strong winds that pass through this land, shaking the garden walls and gates. His visitation was a bit like that! But the buildings are still here. The cross on top of the chapel reaches up, still triumphant! Some lines from his final report follow.

> At New Camaldoli I have found a living community, rich
> with many talents and open, with its ministry of hospitality
> to men and women of today with their problems and also
> with their personal riches and spiritual quests. It is a
> community that is open in many ways to Christian and
> interreligious ecumenism...I can say there is a good spirit
> inside everyone...

Then he spoke of our basic values, and of those of Camaldoli in
Italy:

> ...proposing the foundational values of humanity, the
> Christian Gospel, the monastic life, and specifically the
> Camaldolese charism. And thus the central pillars of our
> spirituality: liturgy, contemplative prayer, *lectio* and serious
> study, community life, hospitality, work, social justice,
> commitment, etc.

He lists in the above some seven 'pillars,' and I am reminded
of the temple that wisdom built, with seven pillars (PROVERBS
9:1). He also wants us to work very hard on founding a rural
monastery here in California, close to the Hermitage, on the
model of the Hermitage and Monastery of Camaldoli which are
just about two miles away from each other. Quite an undertak-
ing for us, both financially and in terms of manpower! Then he
wants us to work more on dialogue! We are a very diversified community, and do need to work on communication and involvement.
But we think that Camaldoli could do some work in this area also.

JULY 31ST

Tonight we gathered again for our poetry seminar, this time
focusing on the work of William Carlos Williams. One of
our young workers has just graduated as an English major from
U.C. Berkeley. He loves Williams and introduced his work and
led the discussion. At first reading, by myself, I did not get
much out of the poems. But with the help and insights of the
others, I have come to be fascinated by his work. I had always
loved his 'Red Wheelbarrow' poem for its Zen-like immediacy
and celebration of things put together rightly, whether in nature or in a finely-crafted poem:

181

so much depends
upon

a red wheel
barrow

glazed with rain
water

besides the white
chickens [97]

Williams does not celebrate just the lovely. He can sing the praises of an old, desperate, drooling woman in terms that remind me of the Song of Songs:

O tongue
licking
the sore on
her netherlip

O toppled belly

O passionate cotton
stuck with
matted hair

elysian slobber
upon
the folded handkerchief

I can't die

—moaned the old
jaundiced woman
rolling her
saffron eyeballs

I can't die
I can't die. [98]

We were struck by the pathos of human decrepitude and decay. That shocking conjunction: 'elysian slobber.' And also the color saffron, with its sacred connotations, to characterize the jaundiced woman's eyeballs. Is her cry, 'I can't die,' repeated three times as a kind of refrain or responsorial verse, simply the expression of the terror of her death? Or could it be her desperation at being locked into a humiliating minimal existence, her frustration that she cannot be released through death? Or is it even, at some mysterious level, the proclamation of her immortality, even in her decrepit state? Is it immortality through the poetic genius of Williams? He does seem to have the capacity to look everything straight-on, to acknowledge and accept the whole thing. And there is an intimation of immortality in that.

AUGUST 6TH
TRANSFIGURATION

Today is a major feast for the Eastern churches, and for all monks, East and West. There is something about that mountain-top experience that is archetypal of the deepest yearnings of every Christian for light, and for transformation in Christ. The Eastern Hesychast Tradition insists that in deep contemplative prayer, we are actually illumined by the light of the Transfigured Christ. The uncreated Taboric Light. In such prayer we are there on the mountaintop with the Apostles, with Moses and Elijah. But, as with the Transfiguration, it is also all in view of suffering, to prepare us for the Cross, and thus we need to descend again into the valley, an inverted mountain.

AUGUST 13TH
SAINTS PONTIAN AND HIPPOLYTUS

Our young monk Cyprian, probably on his way to ordination, preached today. It was a very biblical and liturgical homily, but also quite personal. And only five minutes long! He had obviously worked long on it. It is so much easier to go on and on. Less can truly be more.

+

After Eucharist we processed out to our new generator. We have to produce all our own electricity here, so our hopes are riding on this large, bright yellow machine, that could just barely fit through the generator house door. Bro. Emmanuel, our number one mechanic, who has a way of genius with machines, had

placed a little statue of Mary and a vase of flowers on his new pride and joy, and Cyprian had worked up quite a full liturgy, according to all the rubrics. We paused at the threshold of the generator house for the prayers, but Bro. Emmanuel wanted us right inside, so we dutifully crowded within. The backup machine was running full-blast, so we had to project our collects, hymn, Prayers of the Faithful. I scattered holy water on the engine, wondering if I would short something and cause the whole thing to be sent back for major repair, then generously scattered more holy water on the participants, who, I think, welcomed it in the sweltering confines. Then Emmanuel said we had to conclude everything by starting the motor, which he did, and the huge roar invited us outside the more rapidly. But it was a good liturgy, 'Where the machine meets the cement floor!'

AUGUST 14TH
SAINT MAXIMILLIAN KOLBE

Kolbe is very much a saint for our times. As our Vigils reading put it today, by his offering of his own life in substitution for a poor fellow Dachau prisoner, and then confronting his own death by starvation with such serenity, and comforting the other condemned, he defeated Nazism more profoundly than did the Allied armies.

+

Two of our younger monks are away for medical exams. Like a nervous father, I am awaiting the results. One of the challenges of this job is that I have about twenty-eight kids to think about! And some of them are older than I!

+

Another gem by Williams:

> One day in Paradise
> a Gypsy
>
> smiled
> to see the blandness

185

> of the leaves—
> so many
>
> so lascivious
> and still. [99]

Paradise as the world of the poet, when the poem happens. (Or the world of the contemplative, when the prayer happens). But what is a Gypsy doing in heaven, with all that thieving and lying that they get up to? At most a Gypsy might get into Purgatory. Then again, Jesus had less difficulty with the thieves and prostitutes than with the professional religious and priestly types. Is the Gypsy Williams himself? And why that curious blandness of the leaves? Gypsies are not given to the bland. They might possibly entertain lasciviousness, according to popular stereotypes, but how could there be anything lascivious in Heaven? And how could the lascivious, which implies…agitation, be juxtaposed with 'still?' There is something mysteriously passionate about every seeking of the Ultimate, as well as a profound stillness in the moment of its presence. It all comes together for Williams, like poetic insight or the contemplative experience.

August 15th
The Assumption

There was a wonderful reading at Vigils from Gerald Vann on the Assumption as the reconciliation of Earth and Heaven, of flesh and spirit, so desperately needed in our time. Mary as Mother of God, as Mother of us all, gathering us into one family, and with a glorious, transcendent hope.

> The gulf between matter and spirit, between material things and the praise of God, is widening at a pace and to an extent hitherto unknown: it would be very easy to despair of the civilization of ours…The doctrine of the Assumption is of supreme importance not only to Catholics, but to all men and women, because it means that there is still in the world, there will always be in the world, a voice to affirm and a power to defend the dignity and the ultimate glory of matter, of material things, of human flesh and blood, of the lovely mystery of human love…[100]

Karl Jung says something analogous, that the declaration of the Doctrine of the Assumption is one of the major events of the twentieth century, bringing the feminine right into the Ultimate.

+

Fr. Alessandro of the General's Council phoned this morning, we talked at length (thank heavens they are paying!) about the recent visitation here, and then the broader situation of our Congregation. When I leave for Italy in two weeks, one of the issues I will encounter as Visitator at the mother house of Camaldoli, apparently, is whether the General and Council should give more attention to the mother house, or more to the new foundations in the Third World. The mother house feels drained of manpower and energy. But without that commitment, the Third World houses could be in trouble. Not an easy one to call.

The good news in all this is that the mother house, after almost a thousand years of history, is still alive and kicking, articulate and generative. And also that the Camaldolese, for the first time in that long history, are not only in Italy and the U.S., but also in the Third World, in India and Brazil and (with our nuns) in Africa. This is a small symbol of the universality of the vocation of all God's people to contemplative intimacy and union with God.

CONCLUSION

My Beloved is the Mountains
The solitary wooded valleys
Exotic islands, resounding rivers,
The whisper of amorous breezes.

The tranquil night
At the time of the rising dawn,
Silent music, sounding solitude,
The supper that refreshes and enkindles love.

ST. JOHN OF THE CROSS: THE *SPIRITUAL CANTICLE*

The pages of this chronicle journal have sketched the day-to-day life of the Hermitage. But hopefully they have suggested something more. Eucharist and Divine Office and community moments and encounters with guests want to be for us a 'supper that refreshes.' And we have discovered that the Big Sur mountains and valleys and ocean are charged with the creative presence of the Beloved. And our solitude wants to sound. We listen for the silent music of the Beloved.

And so it is with every Christian, whatever be the specific vocation. For all of us, there is always the primacy of Love, founded on the Gospel, and beyond that, on the very God who is compassionate Love, loving us with abandon, calling forth our love—filial, friendship, and also spousal love. Monks and mystics, honoring the filial and friendship forms of Christian love, have always been attracted in a special way to spousal love as particularly revelatory of our relation with the Beloved. Our favorite book in the Bible tends to be the *Canticle of Canticles*. Our prayers, like the prayers of so many Christians, can turn out to be love songs.

There is a sacred mountain within each of us, and often enough we are absorbed in what is happening in the bustling villages scattered about the mountain, and the ways and byways connecting them. But sometimes we have an intuition, an awareness of what is mysteriously happening at the cloud-wrapped summit.

Here at the Hermitage, as in any Christian household (indeed, as in any Christian heart) daily life has been about getting the chores done, and moments alone, and moments with others, and agreeing and disagreeing, and prayer and rest. And beyond and within it all, Hermitage life and all Christian life are about the silent music. About love on the mountain. About the Beloved.

NOTES

Notes to the Preface

1. Jean Leclercq, O.S.B. *The Love of Learning and the Desire for God: A Study of Monastic Culture*, New York, Fordham University Press, 1977, p.192

2. Quoted by Leclercq, *loc.cit.*

3. Quoted by Leclercq, *loc.cit.* p.194

4. Raimundo Panikkar, et al. *Blessed Simplicity: The Monk as Universal Archetype*, NY, Seabury, 1982 p.11

Notes to the Text

1. Aelred of Rievaulx, *Spiritual Friendship,* Kalamazoo, Michigan, Cistercian Publications, 1977, p.57

2. *Ibid.* pp.72-74

3. *Ibid.* p.60

4. *Ibid.* pp.65-66

5. *Ibid.* pp.131-132

6. *Ibid.* p.75

7. Aelred of Rievaulx, *The Mirror of Charity,* Kalamazoo, Michigan, Cistercian Publications, 1990, p.200 —I have modified the translation to render the English inclusive

8. *Ibid.* p.201

9. See, for instance, Aelred Squire, *Aelred of Rievaulx: A Study,* Kalamazoo, Michigan, Cistercian Publications, 1981

10. Gerald May, *Will and Spirit: A Contemplative Psychology,* San Francisco, Harper & Row, 1982, p.6

11. *Ibid.*

12. *Ibid.* p.36 –May also mentions in this context the book by G. Gordon Liddy, that bears the one-word title, *Will.* The twentieth century has been devastated by the dark will. In desperation many have collapsed into irresoluteness. The only real way out is through the graced humble willingness of the saints.

13. Rollo May, *Love and Will,* New York, W.W. Norton, 1969, p.1 –Quoted in Gerald May, *op.cit.,* p.37

14. St. Teresa, *Life,* trans. John Dalton, Philadelphia, Peter F. Cunningham, 1870, p.166 —Quoted in May's *Will and Spirit,* op.cit., p.37

15. Phyllis Hodgson, *The Cloud of Unknowing and Related Treatises on Contemplative Prayer,* Exeter, Catholic Records Press, 1982, Introduction: xxxix

16. Rudolph of Biberach, *De Septem Itineribus Aeternitatis,* I,1. Quoted in Hodgson, xxxix, n.49

17. *The Cloud of Unknowing,* Ch.4 [I am using my own translation, consulting the Paulist Press, Penguin and Doubleday Image editions].

18. *Ibid.,* Ch.7

19. *Ibid.,* Ch.51

20. *Ibid.,* Ch.49

21. Walsh, *op.cit.,* p.215, n.32

22. *Ibid.*

23. *Ibid.*

24. Julian of Norwich, *Showings, 'Long Text'* Mahwah, New Jersey, Paulist Press, 1978, Ch.53., p.283

25. *Ibid.* Quoted by Edmund Colledge, o.s.a. and James Walsh, s.j. in their Introduction, p.89

26. Walsh in *The Cloud of Unknowing,* p.215 n.321

27. *Showings, op.cit.,* pp.296-297

28. *The Cloud of Unknowing,* Ch.34, Paulist Press edn. pp.185-186

29. Cyprian Vagaggini, *Theological Dimensions of the Liturgy,* Collegeville, Minnesota, Liturgical Press, 1976. –The Liturgical Press also published in 1959 a much abridged version of Cyprian's massive study; but the full work is much richer and many-sided in noting the contemplative depths of authentic liturgical prayer, helping to overcome the liturgy-contemplation dichotomy that so troubled recent centuries of Catholic spirituality.

30. Psalm XIX (20) from the Grail translation, Chicago, GIA Publications, 1993

31. *Ibid.,* Psalm XXV (26)

32. *Ibid.*, Psalm XXVI (27)

33. *Ibid.*,

34. Simon Tugwell O.P., *Ways of Imperfection: An Exploration of Christian Spirituality*, Springfield, Illinois, Templegate, 1985, p.15

35. *Ibid.*, p.16.

36. *Ibid.*

37. Herbert Thurston S.J., and Donald Attwater, ed., *Butler's Lives of the Saints: Complete Edition*, New York, P.J. Kennedy, 1956, vol. I, p.64

38. D.C. Berry, *Poems for Further Reading*, pp.284-85

39. For those who demand the original Gaelic:

>Mise agus Pangur ban
>Duinn ar ndis ni hionann daill;
>Seilig is mian leis sin deghnath
>lem Lem shainceird dom fein gach trath.
>
>Pangur fein a chinneann do
>Modh a shaothair gch aon lo
>Cinnimse mo shain-mhodh fein
>Deacair docht a thabhairt soileir.

40. Rainer Maria Rilke, 'Der Panther,' from *New Poems*, trans. S. Mitchell.

41. 'The Four Winds Council: Statement of Purpose.'

42. *Ibid.*

43. Travis Du Priest, 'Tracking a Spiritual Family History,' in *The Living Church*, January 21, 1996, p.2

44. Mark 3:21

45. Mark 4:8

46. Psalm LX1 (60) *loc.cit.*

47. Matthew 5:3

48. Luke 6:20ff.

49. Luke 18:1

50. Luke 10:41

51. Ranier Maria Rilke, 'The Swan, ' from *New Poems.* –In the rendering here, and in those following, I make use of the translations of S. Mitchell and R. Bly, but also the suggestions of Bro. David and our poetry seminar.

52. Rilke, 'Ich finde dich,' from *A Book for the Hours of Prayer.*

53. Gerard Manley Hopkins, 'God's Grandeur.'

54. Rilke, 'Losch mir die Augen aus,' *loc. cit.*

55. Rilke, 'Ihr vielen unbesturmten Stadte,' from *A Book for the Hours of Prayer.*

56. John Donne, 'Batter My Heart,' from *Holy Sonnets,* n.10

57. Rilke, 'Mein Leben ist diese steile Stunde,' from *A Book for the Hours of Prayer.*

58. *Camaldolese Constitutions and Declaration,* New Camaldoli, California, Hermitage Press, 1985

59. Thomas Matus, o.s.b. Cam., *The Monastic Life of the Camaldolese Benedictines,* New Camaldoli, California, Hermitage Press, 1994

60. Ibid.

61. *The Rule of St. Benedict,* Ch. 1: The Kinds of Monks; 'There are clearly four kinds of monks. First, there are the cenobites, that is to say, those who belong to a monastery, where they serve under a rule and an abbot. Secondly, there are the anchorites or hermits, who have come through the test of living in a monastery for a long time, and have passed beyond the first fervor of monastic life...They have built up their strength and go from the battle line in the rank of their brothers to the single combat of the desert.' —One of Romuald's adaptations of the *Rule* was to encourage some candidates to an immediate encounter with the solitude of the cell, though supported by a community of hermits. He thus restored the ancient laura or skete, a community-of-hermits, a kind of middle way between the cenobium and the isolated hermit.

62. *Ibid.*

63. Matthew 5:17

64. Matthew 5:21

65. Marcia and Jack Kelly, *Sanctuaries: The West Coast and the Southwest,* New York, Bell Tower, 1992, p.12

66. *Ibid.*

67. *Ibid.*

68. *Ibid.*

69. See: I Kings 3:4-13

70. John 2:19,21

71. I Corinthians 6:19

72. Pope Paschal II, Nostris Quidem Temporibus, November 4, 1113; cited in Lino Vigilucci, *Camaldoli: A Journey into its History and Spirituality,* California, Source Books, 1995, p.56

73. Pope John Paul II, Discourse and Homily at Fonte Avellana, September 5, 1982; quoted in *Giovanni Paolo II a Fonte Avellana nel Millenio di Fondazione,* Pesaro, Fonte Avellana, 1982

74. Saint John Chrysostom, homily, *Hom. 6 De Precatione,* PG 64, 462-465.

75. Matthew 5:8

76. Cassian, *Conferences* I:4ff.

77. Matthew 22:30

78. I Corinthians 15:28

79. See, for instance, Evelyn Eaton Whitehead and James D. Whitehead, *Christian Life Patterns: The Psychological Challenges and Religious Invitations of Adult Life,* New York, Crossroad, 1995, pp.79-80, 152-153, etc.

80. Allen Ginsberg, *Howl and other Poems,* San Francisco, City Lights Books. 1973, p.9

81. T.S. Eliot, *op.cit.,* p.191

82. Mark 12:28-34 [Gospel for Friday of the Third Week of Lent].

83. Oliver Clement, *The Roots of Christian Mysticism,* London, New City Press, 1993, p.76

84. Cf. T.S. Eliot, *op.cit.,* p.191

85. *An Ancient Homily on Holy Saturday,* PG 43, 439ff.

86. Melito of Sardis, *An Easter Homily,* SC 123, 120ff.

87. Thomas Keating, 'The Two Streams of Cenobitic Tradition in the RSB,' in *Cistercian Studies 4,* 1976

88. Quoted in Richard Davenport-Hines' *Auden,* New York, Pantheon, 1995, p.112

89. T.S. Eliot, 'The Family Reunion,' in *The Complete Poems and Plays,* New York, Harcourt Brace, 1971, p.281

90. Quoted in Richard Davenport-Hines' *Auden, op.cit.,* p.158

91. I have modified the translation offered in Angelus Silesius, *The Cherubinic Wanderer,* Mahwah, New Jersey, Paulist Press, 1986

92. W.B. Yeats, 'The Second Coming.'

93. Thomas Merton, *Conjectures of A Guilty Bystander,* New York, Image, 1968, p.158

94. *Ibid.,* p.19

95. 'De Pace,' PL 52, 347-348

96. *Catechism of the Catholic Church,* Rome, Libreria Editrice Vaticana, 1994, p.588, n.2448

97. William Carlos Williams, *The Collected Poems I,* New York, New Directions, 1986, p.224

98. *Ibid.,* pp.215-216

99. *Ibid.,* p.223

100. Gerald Vann, *The Water and the Fire,* pp.175-176